God of the Splitsecond

Unusual Events or Coincidences

by

TRUDY MORROW

PRESS

Dedication

This book is dedicated to the grandchildren of the Strauss Family, and especially to my niece Anita whose idea it was to have me write these stories down for their children. Most of these live in Germany, and I am working on the translation of this storybook for them.

Acknowledgement

The book cover was created by my friend Hannah R. Walsh, a young graphic artist, who did such a great job on her computer. My gratitude also to the many friends who encouraged me to share this family book with the public.

I am grateful for the permission given to me by the Galizien Hilfskommitee to use the two lino cuts by Rudolf Unterschütz of the caravan and the colonists resting under the oak. The name "Hilfskomitee" is the correct spelling in German.

My special thanks to Peter and Elfrieda Dyck, who gave me permission to paraphrase their epic event of the "Berlin Exodus through the Red Sea" in their task to help over a thousand Mennonites escape in 1947 in a freight train from the Soviet zone to go to Paraguay, South America. The authors' book entitled "Up from the Rubble" was published by Herald Press, 1991.

GOD-OF-THE-SPLITSECOND
Unusual Events or Coincidents

One generation shall praise thy works to another,
and shall declare thy mighty acts, o Lord.
King James Bible (Psalm 145,4)

This book was originally written for the grandchildren of our family interspersed with my personal memoirs and the history of our ancestors. Each story has a number and a title for easy reading and I added drawings to each story. It reminds me of a string of pearls, mixed with different bobbles and shapes to highlight a pattern.

The book starts with "Emma on the Road", the first event I remember as a 11-year old that God had something to do with this event in 1945, when among the hundreds of refugees my mother's cousin happened to walk by among the wagons on an unknown road, hundreds of miles away from home.

I derived the title of the book from an event that happened "50 years and 5 seconds later" and I call it "Babushka in the Field" from which I coined the title of my book. An old woman standing by the roadside, when a busload of West Germans were trying to visit their homeland and villages after the collapse of Communism. They couldn't find their village since names had been changed. That babushka hopped on their bus and led the driver to our town. It happened that she knew my grandfather as well.

Also, I found "God-of-the-Splitsecond" stories in other people's lives and included these as well, such as Corrie ten Boom; Squanto, the Cape Cod Indian, the Schaeffers and L'Abri, Switzerland and others. The most dramatic was the escape of 1200 Mennonites from the Soviet-occupied city of Berlin in an US Army freight train in 1947. What God can do for one family, he demonstrates in countless others.

The book covers the period from World War II in 1945 to the Twin Towers 9-11 event in New York in 2001. And when I considered the story of our family, I came up with a trilogy of images, such as:

-- three caravans, -- three ships, --three centuries,

I learned that my own generation and lifespan covers three distinct centuries, because we are the first ones in human history to have gone through such vast and rapid changes in one lifetime.

19th Century– the field and the oil lamp -*agriculture*
20th Century– the electricity and the assembly line - *industry*
21st Century– the atom bomb and the computer chip - *hi-tech*

Trudy Strauss Morrow

Table of Contents

Part I

Family Life and
Personal Journey

*T*he story starts with *"Emma on the Road"* as the first
event I can remember as a child seeing God in action.
The other story equally as amazing is "Babushka in the
Field", which happened 50 years and 5 seconds later, from
which I coined the word "God-of-the-Splitsecond".

In this section of the book I have woven in various
reflections on our past and the journey of our ancestors in
caravans, in order to paint the background of the journey
we were called to make as a family between captivity
and freedom, war and peace, earthly trials and heavenly
blessings.

Here I also describe that although I went to Canada on
a ship to scout out the territory for our refugee family who

was eager to follow, things turned out differently and they decided to stay in West Germany and settle there. I was led to enter college, expecting to end up on a missionfield as a translator, but landed in Germany instead.

Please note the trilogy of themes:
* three caravans * three ships * three centuries

1. Emma on the Road (main story)

B ack in the winter of 1945 on an icy bitter-cold January morning we found ourselves as part of a long caravan of refugees on a road in Pommern (East Germany) trying to escape from the Soviet Army which was steadily pushing ahead, while the receding Nazi Army was trying to hold them back for us civilians. Some days we were only 10 to 15 miles away from the fighting front. At night, while we slipped into an empty, cold house just to get a few naps of sleep or to find some food, we could see the red glowing horizon of burning towns or villages. How long, before the enemy will catch up with us?

One event stayed as clear in my mind as if it happened yesterday and I call it "Emma On The Road". We were all women folk on this old wagon (the men including my father had been drafted to war). The estate owner (Gutsbesitzer) of our town let people take any vehicle and horse team to escape from the oncoming Russians, before he and his family took off in his car. Our "donated" wagon was drawn by two heavy-weight field horses, they were perhaps 20 or 25 years old. We took only the most necessary things so as

17

to leave enough room for twelve people: my Aunt Erna, her five children and her mother, and my mother Lola with us four daughters. Luckily, my mother was raised as a farmer's daughter and knew how to handle horses, while Aunt Erna was a city lady, her husband being the principal of the high school in town. And "Oma", the grandmother of my cousins, played the role of nanny to all of us nine children.

On that particular day, the old horses acted up, we had trouble moving on and eventually pulled over to the side of the road, while the caravan of refugees on loaded horse-drawn wagons and people walking alongside kept passing us. Our horses were so stubborn, they just stood there and mother tried all she knew to get them going. We became more worried, should we give up our vehicle and beg other refugees to take us with them? But who would want to add twelve helpless people to their load?

All of a sudden, I heard my mother scream "Oh, Emma, Emma!" She had recognized her cousin among the by-passers, a tall young lady walking besides her folks' wagon. I can still see them in my mind, my mother and Emma hugging each other. When Mom asked, "Where is your baby?" she replied, "Oh, it died just a few days ago, we had to bury it in the snow in the ditch." As refugees, there was no time to find a cemetery or a minister of a town along the road, people had left before them, so they made a grave by the roadside. But then Emma pulled herself away from mother and ran to catch up with her family wagon before she would loose sight of it.

My imagination as an eleven year old completed the picture of this encounter of the two ladies, and I thought, "Maybe God had to slow us down, so we would see Emma, and that mother could hug her and pray with her to encourage her." I was too young to anticipate the miraculous encounter as an act of God and what He had to do before this scene would pass before my eyes. These two women were friends and neighbors in our homeland in Galicia (Poland), but were uprooted from their village in 1939 by the Nazis and forcefully relocated to live in different regions of the Warthegau. They hadn't seen each other for a long time.

To compound the problem, we were part of a stream of thousands of refugees traveling different uncharted routes, and we were hundreds of miles away from home. It would have been something like you were traveling along an unknown road in New Jersey, while your cousin lived in Massachussets and ended up on the same road by accident? Just to run into your cousin like that is no coincidence, but a sheer act of the *God-of-the-Splitsecond*. This encounter would not have happened, if we had chosen another route or had not been delayed by lazy horses, etc. No chance for a coincidence.

Babushka in the Field (significant event, see story #62)

The most dramatic *God-of-the-Splitsecond* event, in my opinion, is this one, because of the unusual circumstances surrounding it and the timing, namely 50 years and 5 seconds later, as I call it. I named the title of this book by this event.

It happened in the spring of 1991, when a busload of Germans went on a tour to their homeland in Eastern Europe (Poland and the Ukraine) which had been under Soviet control for fifty years since 1940 and had been inaccessible since that time. Hitler then forcefully removed hundreds of thousands of ethnic Germans from their homeland, and our family was among these. We were put into freight trains like cattle (or chattels?) and relocated by the Nazis into one of the empty Polish homes, from which they previously deported the Poles or Jews and sent to German labor camps. However, our forced stay in the Warthegau (captured Poland) was only brief, because five years later in 1945 we had to flee from the Russian front to West Germany.

So none of us had seen our original homeland in Galizia since 1940. The memory of the Germans in our homeland had been erased by changing town names and removing records, the Communists (Soviets) took away anything worthwhile, even frames of houses, machinery, bricks, etc. and shipped it to Russia. Then they combined the whole village into one huge "kolchos". Each farmhouse had only a tiny yard, maybe 30 feet deep. The rest of their land was taken from them and they became laborers in the kolchos.

Here in 1991 is this busload of people trying to visit their towns and villages after 50 years. My cousin Lilly and her husband were among them and they had maps and photos with them. The bus driver who organized this trip was Polish. He was driving along dirt roads trying to find our village named "Theodorshof" or the current Polish equivalent name. But they found no signs and the road along fields was muddy and bumpy, no blacktop roads yet. In the distance they saw an old woman, what we call "Babushka" with her headscarf carrying a large basket with vegetables and walking along the road. The bus driver stopped and asked her in Polish: "Babushka, where is the town of ......?" A puzzled look – maybe the name of the town had been changed in the meantime, the driver thought.

But my cousin had the presence of mind, she leaned out the doorway and called in German "Where are the graves of Strauss and Mueller?" (which were our mutual grandfathers). The bus driver translated this into Polish, when the old woman beamed and pointed excitedly to an overgrown hill at the end of the field. The driver asked her to step inside the bus, so that she could guide them along. "Oh, you are his grandchild? I remember Mr. Strauss and also Mr. Mueller very well, I grew up in the same village." They also learned that Babushka was one of the two families who had NOT been evacuated by the Soviets from that town and replaced by strangers in the Communist shuffle of relocating people.

Here are the amazing facts: If the bus had taken another route or some another road, they would not have met Babushka. If Babushka had decided to go to the field on another day, or at a different hour, they would not have met her. Was it just a coincidence that SHE was there, and not just any stranger or neighbor from town? Can you see God in action, fifty years and five seconds later? This event was just as good as if I had been there in person instead of my cousin, and it tells me that the God of History is the God of Providence, the One who loves and cares for me and for you. Praise be to the *God-of-the-Splitsecond!*

These two events are the nucleus to my writing this book for our grandchildren. In fact, I coined the word "splitsecond" from this Babushka story. Next, a glimpse at the life we lived for generations in Eastern Europe established by our ancestors in 1783. You may want to skip this section and continue with the "Exodus to Captivity" section beginning with story # 5.

2. Caravan to Galizia by Colonists anno 1782

While farmers and others in the United States moved westward on their horse and wagon along with other homesteaders to claim new land, there were families in Europe who moved eastward in the opposite direction to establish homes. The plague and crowded communities had made it difficult to live there. My ancestors from the Rheinland-Pfalz and the Black Forest in Germany were also heading for Eastern Europe.

The Pfalz was a beautiful rich region with vineyards, apple orchards and fields on the sloping hills. Among them were our great-great-great great grandparents named "Strauss", seven generations back, who together with other villagers from the Pfalz were offered to establish a new colony in the fertile farmland of Galizia near Lvow at the friendly invitation of Empress Katharina the Great, wife of Czar Peter I. Being of German royalty she wanted to have some good settlers from her home country rather than the flighty Cossack nomads in the virgin woodlands, who usually had a bonfire and a dance and then moved on.

One of the documents showed a settlement agreement dated September 17, 1781 signed by Joseph II, the Ruler of Holy Roman Empire, and with the King in Lvow, Galizia, granting religious freedom and a tax-exempt status to the colonists to build their home and trades in the new territory. About 15,000 people joined those homesteader caravans to the East and established about 194 villages in the new homeland. Often neighbors in the old land settled next to their old relatives or friends again.

It is these people who established thriving agricultural communities and ethnic villages and towns, furthered education and medicine, built schools, hospitals, and established trade- and art guilds. The city of Lvow was known for its beautiful architecture and the textile industry, in particular. They were subjects of the Austrian-Hungarian Empire until World War I.

The next several stories are recollections of our past genera-
tions and our original homeland in Galizia. They illustrate
the kind of community we had and paint a better picture of
the events leading to our deportation by Hitler in the winter
of 1939-40 to the Warthegau after he defeated Poland
in a two-week war. Thus we became subjects of Hitler's
Great Reich and his plan was to claim thousands of ethnic
Germans, remove them from their homeland and place them
into homes of Poles or Jews whom he sent to labor camps.
The final objective of this unsettling and moving of our peo-
ples was to draft all eligible men to war.

This section also refers to our Flight from our assigned home
in Poland just five years later in 1945 as the Soviets were
approaching (see "Emma on the Road"). Please note that
people fled from their homes and escaped either on foot or on
a horse-driven wagon, if they were fortunate to get one in that
crisis. Although the invention of the famous "Volkswagen",
the car with the motor in the back trunk, which was pro-
duced during Hitler's time, it was not available to most of
the citizens inspite of its name "people's car". They could
not afford one or get one, only the military, the government
and special people, like doctors, had a Volkswagen. And they
drove that "wonder" on the Autobahn (highway) also cre-
ated by the Nazis especially for the Volkswagen, an occa-
sional Mercedes or some trucks.

3. Village Life on the Bauernhof

Our village, called Theodorshof, was one of those typical German-speaking towns established by the original colonists in the 18th century, and I was born on the farm which
my ancestors built about seven generations earlier.

Legend says that colonists were offered a square kilo-
meter of virgin woodland for one gold dollar "Taler" and
they were subjects of the Austrian-Hungarian Empire. These

settlers cut their own wood and built houses and barns, established and cultivated fields.

If you can picture a straight mud road as main street, dirt paths on either side and trees along the way for shade. There were picket fences along the road, because one farm joined the next and the houses stood in a neat row, wooden whitewashed houses with heavy straw-thatched roofs and with overlapping eves, like a brim of a hat to protect them from rain. On many rooftops were stork nests with permanent occupants. These birds came back to the same address every spring.

Perhaps you know what a straw-thatched Danish house looks like. Ours were similar. However, in the rigid Eastern winter, the farmer stacked bundles of straw around the outside wall up to 3 feet high and 1 foot thick for protection from the cold. Mother said, the house needed warm socks for the winter. In the springtime that straw was taken to the barn for the animals. And instead, many colorful perennial flowers showed up in the soil around the house.

When mother sent me on an errand to the grocer to buy some salt or other items, I would hold the money pouch in one hand and a long stick in the other with which I would tap each picket fence to create a rhythm as I ran alongside. Then I would vary the music and scrape three fence posts, skip one, and repeat the pattern. All of us kids in town liked that "rap game", quite different from what you hear today from bands. Some grandmother might look out of the window to see what kid was making that racket.

Or in our playtime we were allowed to run to the "Dorflinde" (the big village tree) which had benches and worn out grass around it because it was a meeting ground for the villagers. In the hot summer we kids ran a little farther down to the creek for a cool swim. Perhaps our village life in Eastern Europe reminds you of "Huckleberry Finn".

There was another common ground, the Bake House, a one-room structure built just for baking, but there was no baker, instead it belonged to the village for anyone to use. The women used this in the summer time to save heating up their house with their own oven. Our fireplace was a comfortable warm space with benches on either side and a tall pizza-like oven with a space in the upper part for baking and heating. The cat preferred that warm spot on the bench or she settled on top of the oven.

Saturday mornings was baking time, when the women would carry the rising dough in their wooden bowls under their arm to that Bake House. They had their daughters help them with the other necessary stuff, like flour, dried fruits etc. and pull this along in a little cart. The oven was like a pizza oven and the women could place their bread dough and their braided white bread or cakes in there and bring some mending along to chat with the other women while waiting for the baking to be done.

Saturday afternoon was set aside to prepare for Sunday, the day of rest, and they meant it. The house and barns were cleaned up, even the front stops were scrubbed and washed clean by the kids. The men or boys had the chores of sweeping the yard and raking the soil in neat long rows. It looked so tidy that you'd hate to leave your footprints in the raked sand.

Another thing to do for the kids was to polish everyone's leather shoes (white sneakers were unheard of) and to pick out the clothes we would wear to walk to church. Girls would always wear dresses, of course, and nobody wore jeans to church. Instead, they dressed up in their Sunday best.

Then there was our Lutheran church with a tall steeple and the schoolhouse next to it because our "Pfarrer" (pastor) was also the teacher at the German school during the week in the same building. And we had bells in the church tower which rang every day almost like a "town clock". It was the duty of some boy or confirmand to pull those bell strings in the morning "time for school", at noon, in the evening "time to stop work", on Sunday, "time to worship".

In fact, the bell defined all of our lives, birth, marriage, death, celebrations as well as calamity.

Quiet Riot in the Village

But I should mention another change in our village. When my mother's cousin went to Germany as a young man to learn a mechanics trade, he was boarding at the home of his Master-guildsman whose family was Pietist, people who believed in conversion and a holy life of discipleship. This young man eventually felt called to the ministry and traveled around many communities. Several persons in our village accepted the Lord Jesus Christ into their hearts and were baptized. My mother was one of them. They called them Anabaptists.

When the preacher came to our town, our home was open for Bible studies. However, the Lutheran husbands of some of the women planned an attack to chase this man out of town. They'd yell and holler outside or drag one or the other woman out of the room. One night they came to our house with the intention of breaking windows. Apparently the meeting was not held there that night. And they were so angry to have missed the group, that they threw some stones into the window anyway.

When mother came home, she found me in my crib near the window sleeping peacefully, while some glass pieces rested on top of me. Could an angel have held back the assault? She was amazed at that protection and I can't help but wonder. I believe that *God-of-the-Splitsecond* sent some guardians to protect this baby.

4. Oma Elisabeth and Her Rocking Chair

I was only six years old, when we were deported from our homeland Galizia, but I still have vivid memories of our village life and especially of grandma and grandpa's big farm in another town called Sabiezanka, about 10 miles away from our village of Theodorshof. It was a treat for me when our family traveled in a horse carriage (no cars then) to visit them. Sometimes I was allowed to stay with Oma for a week or two. Then someone would bring me back, or my parents would come to get me.

I remember Oma as a delicate tiny lady, who always wore a dark colored gingham dress with floral print or polka dots. She was a neat as her handmade dress. She wore a white apron when she worked in the kitchen to cook a meal for her large family. Her hair was neatly arranged in the back with a braid twisted in a bun. She was always helpful and friendly and hummed some tunes while she was working. No radio in those days.

From Oma I learned what a "Dämmerstündchen" is, which means "little dusk hour". It was the time before supper in which she relaxed, having put all the pots with vegetables, potatoes, and whatnot on the wood stove. While she sat in her rocking chair within reach to put a few more logs into the fire, there was no lamp burning. It wasn't dark enough for the oil lamp and would be wasteful as she told me. This was the time for me to sit on a little footstool or sit on her lap, and listen to her tell me a story while we waited for dinner to cook. Nobody else was in the room, her daughters and her son were all busy in the barn, feeding the animals and milking the cows.

In that lovely, memorable dusk hour, I got my religious instruction, at least what I remember. Oma was Lutheran and she knew her catechism by heart. So I learned "the first commandment" etc. But what I enjoyed most was listening to her lovely high voice, singing many hymns that she had memorized like "Ein feste Burg ist unser Gott", and other folk songs. Or I'd ask her to sing me a favorite song or tell me a story, or show me the famous pictures and rhymes of "Max und Moritz" by Wilhelm Busch, as popular to us as "Charlie Brown" is to Americans.

I also remember one night, when Oma may have heard me tossing and turning in my bed nearby. She called over to me, "Traudi, why aren't you sleeping?" I don't know, but I had an answer that amuses me still today. I said to my grandmother: "Oma, I am counting the time!" What I really said in German: "Oma, ich muss die Zeit zählen!" I could hear Oma's big alarm clock on the dresser making "tick, tock, tick, tock," and that's what captivated me. Apparently we didn't have such a loud alarm clock in my parents' house.

In some of those waking moments I could hear Oma sigh, "Ach, lieber Herrgott!" which means "Oh, Lord God!" I didn't know what she meant, but I understand now, she must have been praying silently on her bed next to the sleeping Opa, but once in a while she emphasized her plea with that phrase.

In the Evening after supper, the family would gather around the fireplace and read a story out loud or we would sing, while someone played a tune on the mandolin or the violin. The women folk would mend clothes or knit, crochet or play board games. There was plenty of handwork to do. Maybe one of the daughters spun wool on the spinning wheel. Even weaving and rug hooking was routine activity, or sewing dresses, shirts, about everything you wore was handmade, except the tailored suit or coat. The men even knew how to repair our shoes. So there was no time to waste. Home life in those days was a family industry, even leisure time was work, but they made work their play, and they had a positive attitude.

The Babysitting Tree

I remember another scene from my childhood, babysitting under a tree. My father and mother had to plow the fields and plant potatoes. The fields were right behind our barn, but they were long leading down a slope to a creek. Babysitters were not always available because the other people had to work too. So Mama set up a basket with our baby under the shadow of a tree and put me on a blanket next to it with some toys and a bottle of milk for the baby and something for me to nibble and drink.

It was funny how Mama knew how to keep my spirits up so that I would not feel deserted and lonely. As she walked behind Papa, who guided the horse and the plow to make furrows for the potatoes, mother threw the potato chunks into the soil rhythmically, but she kept waving at me with one hand and call to me, "Yoohoo, Traudi, I am here!" And as my parents and the horse got smaller in the distance, I could still hear mother calling to me. And then as they turned around, this working team became larger and larger, until they stopped at the babysitting tree.

By the way, my father was studying in Bielitz near Krakau as a young man to become teacher, when his dad, my grandfather Rudolf Strauss, suddenly became ill with pneumonia and died. His mother had to ask her son to come home and take over the farm, because his brothers were married and had families and farms of their own. Ours was the original colony homestead founded in the 18th century. Soon my grandmother married again and moved away, and so my father and mother had no one else to help them with the farm. But they managed, at harvest time they hired some help from the next village.

Our original colonists were under the rule of the Austrian-Hungarian Empire, then the Polish took possession in World War I and in September 1939, Hitler defeated Poland, gave Stalin our villages and took us away to "The Reich". It may sound sad, but I am told, the other alternative would have been for us to be shipped by Stalin to Siberia.

Village Life

Life for us was typical village life, and they say that a person's life centered around what distance he could cover from sunrise to sunset, even when traveling by horse and buggy. And that lifestyle went from generation to generation almost unchanged. The villagers shared in each other's lives and enjoyed each other's company. It was like one big family, you didn't need a special invitation to come and visit. Special occasions, like a wedding, were a village affair and they celebrated for several days. Everyone shared in food, made special dishes, brought them along, so that the host-family would not become impoverished.

At Easter the church choir presented special chorus pieces, orchestrated by the local musicians. Pentecost had another tradition. The young eligible bachelors competed, as to who would rise first and ride on his horse to get to the "Dorflinde" (village tree) first. The guy who slept in became the laughing stock of the town. May-Day was a celebration around a tall tree pole. One of the men climbed up to the top and fastened a big wreath with a handful of long colorful ribbons. As they dangled down, boys and girls would each grab one ribbon and dance around the pole. My grandfather's farm was generally the meeting ground for the young people to get together, socialize and make music with their instruments. They loved to sing and they had so much fun and wit to entertain themselves.

There was child labor. Nobody thought that work would kill you, not back then. Depending upon the age and maturity of the child, boy or girl, they would bring in a pale of water from the well and help with cleaning. The girls were part of the laundry team, helping mother with the chores. No washing machine, but scrubbing the linens on the old washboard and wringing them by hand like a long rope, twisting until the water was squeezed out. At other times, the kids were expected to help feeding the cows, pigs, chicken, or horses. The older kids had to lead the cows to the meadow, i.e. drive a herd and follow with a stick in the hand while the dog trotted along. Then that kid had to stay out there in the meadow until it was time to come home in the evening. How is that for an assignment? My mother was a "cowgirl" in her younger days. Have you heard the word "Gänsemagd"? (translated "goose maid"). Older boys or girls had to herd the gees, or goats. sheep, or whatever.

Another chore needed at harvest time was to take the food which mother or grandmother prepared and carry it by hand to the people working in the field. It was usually some healthy delicious soup, bread and sausage, and some fruit compot. No fresh apples all year around, but dried fruits made into a stew. The food deliverer also brought a canister with fresh cold water to drink. Then he or she would cover it in the shade, so that the harvest workers could have a cool drink when they were thirsty.

Babysitting or looking after your siblings was also the responsibility of the older child, if there was no grandmother around who would take care of them. This was needed during the daytime, when the parents had to work in the field, not at night. But there were some rewards to all of this, they received lots of love and caring. And they had time to play and explore their neighborhood.

The No-List

It would take a whole chapter to list all the things those people didn't have and didn't need either. The stuff we are burdened with that we must have, and when we get it, the excitement soon fades and we look for another thing to fill the emptiness of our lives.

Well, let me count a few items these people didn't have:

no car	no electricity
no telephone	no cell phone
no television	no radio
no computers	no copiers
no washing machines	no hair dryers
no noisy store music	no surveillance
no strawberries in winter	no fresh salad in winter
no drive-in restaurants	no telemarketing
no ready made clothes	no throwaway shoes
no busses	bicycles, maybe

but more peace of mind!

Seasons of Life

You might think of the Walt Disney Film "Circle of Life" depicting animal life in Africa. But that is not quite true of the vision our ancestors had of life. True, there was a "time to sow and a time to reap". But we don't go in circles, we go forward, onward, upward to a purposeful goal. We are living, working, and moving between the "Alpha" and the "Omega" of our Lord. We are part of the "Light and Glory" of HIS-STORY, regardless, whether in some small obscure community or in a famous place.

Those villagers lived their daily lives in the light of eternity. Death was not the end of things, but a gateway to heaven. We did not have fancy funeral homes. Our deceased were placed in an open coffin in the hallway of our house. No secret, no cover up, children could see them. As those church bells rang, it rang out a somber, yet joyful message:

"In that Great Kingdom Morning, Fare Thee Well"
and an 'Aufwiedersehen' in the world to come.

In the pages above I described village life of our ancestors in our homeland Galiza, which they created from virgin wood-

land back in 1783, after leaving their homes in Rheinland-Pfalz as colonists traveling eastward. Entire villages joined on this endeavor together and formed the first caravan of settlers. But in 1939 Hitler confiscated their lands and possessions and generously gave them to Stalin for exchange of the ethnic people, because he wanted to draft all men to war and for other plans he had unbeknownst to us.

5. Exodus to Captivity

While I painted the scenario of our peaceful village life in our homeland, where our people lived for about 150 years, I want to bring you back to the reality of our forced removal by Hitler and his Nazi regime in the winter of 1939-40, a big campaign which they called "Heim ins Reich". That dictator gave our land and all possessions to Stalin without our approval, because he needed the ethnic German people for his army unbeknownst to us. And father consoled us with the thought, that we might have been shipped by Stalin to a Siberian labor camp instead.

In the winter of 1939-40 we had to leave our village Theodorshof, and all able men were to join the caravan of tent-covered wagons on icy country roads instead, there were no tar-covered roads then. My father was one of the men and he wore a long sheepskin coat with earflaps. The winters in Eastern Europe can be brutal.

There were no McDonald's Restaurants or Holiday Inns on the way. You had to sustain yourself on the loaf of broad and sausage or dried fruit that you brought with you. There were no tall light posts along the way, only the oil lamps dangling from the caravan wagons, like the New England candles in the windows giving the passerby some light. And when it got dark, the men had to stop their horses, cover them with a heavy blanket, while they crawled inside their covered wagon for some hurried sleep.

Folks like my father who were ordered by the Nazis to leave their village and to "come home to the Reich", which was Hitler's great idea of a New World Order back then in 1940. Entire villages were evacuated by the SS (like Nazi Marines, so to speak). The displaced folks didn't know where they would end up. Only the SS soldiers riding on motorcycles alongside the caravan new where they were taking them to.

My father was on the caravan by himself. His wife and four children were among those women, children and old or sick people being transported in crowded freight trains for about six months, neither of them knowing where the other part of the family was. The people in those freight trains were moved from camp to camp. Sometimes the train stalled for a day or two with those people being cooped up in the windowless train sitting on the straw-covered floor. At mealtime the soldiers brought some thin soup or make-believe coffee to the tracks outside and handed it to the people holding out a tin can or pewter plate.

These train-refugees were eventually united with those coming on the caravan, among them being our father. After a couple of weeks on the hard winter road, the men were ordered to hand in their wagons and horses and all the stuff they loaded on it for safekeeping. All that was actually confiscated by them at the end of that arduous trip. That was a great disappointment, to be robbed of the little bit of possessions they saved from their homeland.

Meanwhile, we folk in the freight train were still shuttled from camp to camp, while the Nazis were emptying the homes of Jewish and Polish occupants and sending them to labor camps. Today we would call this ordeal ethnic cleansing, it was the most cruel action of a godless dictator. None of this I understood at that time as a six-year old girl. But since these tragic events were retold in our homes over the years, I eventually got the picture. I also learned that hundreds of those train-refugees died in an epidemic of colds and other diseases. My grandfather, my cousin and others were among the dead. Their bodies were unable to take the rough treatment in the cold freight cars and the miserable food we received. Most of us children were put into an infirmary hospital. We had contacted some contagious disease and our parents could only wave to us from the outside, while we pressed our noses against the window pane. What agony that must have been for us! And another price we paid for the uprooting, four of my uncles were drafted to war, only one of them returned.

Showers of Disgrace

I remember another scene, a shower of disgrace. We women and children were shoved along the bleak hallway to a large room that had a row of shower heads sticking out of the wall. This camp used to be an army barrack at one time, but it was unsuitable for women and children. My mother was given some soap and a towel and we had to undress and drop our clothes on the floor. No private bathrooms, no curtains, but clusters of people under each of those shower faucets – stark naked. As a six-year old girl, I didn't comprehend the extent of humiliation which my mother and the other womenfolk must have endured as civilized and chaste persons to be exposed and treated like cattle.

I remember my mother pointing her finger at me and saying: "Traudi, don't you ever forget that we are children of the Most High!" I didn't understand how deeply she must have been hurt. Much less, would she understand our present cultural violations of "co-ed bathrooms and showers" at some of our colleges today? Remember the uproar which three devout Jewish students caused at Yale University a few years ago? As Freshmen they had to live in the dormitory and use those co-ed bathrooms which apparently had no curtains. That requirement was against their moral upbringing.

We maintain a code of privacy even at our homes, don't we? Well, Yale University wouldn't let the three Jewish boys study, but due to the national outrage they were eventually permitted to live with their parents nearby or in an apartment in town.

Assigned Home in The Reich

Eventually, after six months of being shuttled back and forth in those freight trains, we were united as a family, we had only a few bundles of clothes. Father had to give up the wagon with the horses and all the possessions he had brought along. We were brought to a town near Lodz (Poland) by the officials. Our family was finally reunited in a little Polish town and brought to our new residence that must have belonged to some evacuated Jews or Poles before us. Now standing on the steps of a two-story house on Main Street, the official said: "Herr Strauss, this is going to be your new home." No questions asked or permitted, shall I say. I learned eventually that father had pretended to have a nervous breakdown. When given some options of what occupation to take, he asked for permission of being grocer. He told us after the War that "bread and butter is neutral. All of us need to eat." He thus escaped the treacherous task of being appointed teacher in the Nazi regime.

Being a grocer can be fun, but not when you had to follow all kinds of regulations passed down to you by the government. For one thing, all sales personnel in our grocery story had to wear clean white lab coats. Each sale had to be accounted for by clipping coupons: coupons for butter, bread, sugar, even sewing thread, anything. We children spent our evening hours matching those coupons and pasting them with flour paste onto large sheets of newspapers. These became the shopping lists for Papa's next purchase.

There were some benefits though, maybe we took advantage of our grocer-dad. When boxes of cherries, blueberries, and other fruit arrived and were stored in the storage room next to our kitchen, we would sneak in and steal a handful of these goodies, run downstairs to the backyard and relish these sweet fruits. As we spit out the kernels onto the pebble walk, we thought that was it. How come Dad discovered the tiny pits lateron and held us accountable?

6. Jewish Bread Basket with a Psalm

German people had more and better coupons on their monthly food rations, while Polish- and Jewish customers had second class rations. Somehow, father found a way to stack some things on a side for a family in need. And when the Jewish people in our town were locked inside a ghetto, things became really bad. One day, mother talked to me in a serious mood, "Now Traudi, don't you breathe a word to anyone where I am going to take you too. Promise!"

She packed a basket with bread, butter and some other things and took me along the back alleys, and we walked zigzag through the neighborhood, so that they wouldn't find out about our visit. We arrived at an old woman's cottage. After greeting her, mother placed the food on the table and talked to that sick woman. Then mother said, "Let's read a psalm!" Next, the Jewish woman chanted her psalm in Hebrew, and my mother sang her version of it. I believe it was the 23. Psalm. I stood in the doorway just observing that scene. You see, I had already been indoctrinated by my Nazi teachers not to believe this Bible stuff since I am a child of the "New Age". That was 60 years ago back in 1942.

In my mind, I lived on the fence, so to speak. In school the teacher asked me, if my parents pray with me and read the Bible at home. But if I would tell her the truth, my parents could get into trouble. On Sunday mornings they took me along obscure paths through fields and meadows to a secret house meeting where believers who went "underground" would show up as scattered individuals and at different times of the day just to share with others in prayer and worship. Some of them knew hymns in Russian. I listened intently to the deep sad melodies which these people sang in a strange language.

However, on Monday morning the teacher knew exactly who was not present at the Hitler Youth sports meeting at 10:00am. I was one of them and had to pay One Reichsmark (like one dollar) as punishment plus hear a humiliating lecture in front of the class.

Another sad event that comes to my mind. The entire school was asked to come in uniform the next day, and we marched in classes to the market square. In front of us were 5 gallows and 5 Jewish men hanging up high, waiting to be executed. I didn't know at that time, that the entire Jewish Ghetto was ordered to go to the square and watch this event too, and that family members had to pull the rope!

I was so horrified, but afraid to show my shock. When I came home, I hid my head in mother's skirt and cried. "What happened?" she asked, but I could barely tell her. You see, I lived before television. I had never seen any one being shot, murdered, or any other violence. And to unexpectedly live through a horrible event like that?! Mother's answer: "Child, they do this to frighten us so we would be scared and obey them. But our God is able to deliver us."

You see, I can't imagine how fearful our lives would have been without my parent's faith and trust in the Almighty. Although in my teens I strayed far away, thinking my pious folk were a handicap to enjoying life to the fullest. Well, well, I eventually grew up after my own wilderness wanderings of faith.

Our visit to that sick lady with our bread basket was the last one. The entire Jewish area in our town became fenced-in and inaccessible as a Ghetto. Jews were not allowed to walk on our sidewalks but on the street, wearing that yellow David-star on their chest. Soon afterwards we saw wagonload after wagonload of Jews transported through town to get to a "labor camp" as we were told, but it was really to a concentration camp - destination "Holocaust".

The last tragedy which some people observed was the move by the SS officers of about 3000 Jewish people which they cramped into the sanctuary of our Roman Catholic church and kept there for a week with hardly any food or water, while they took daily truckloads to that infamous "labor camp" Auschwitz. As they emptied out the sanctuary, they said that two Jews must be still in the building. They looked everywhere, but couldn't find them. Those two young men hid, one in the crevice of the roof, the other on top the beams of the bell tower and they were not found. They escaped from the rooftop and made it to the West to tell the story. One of them was Abraham Ziegler, whom my sister and her husband met in Tel Aviv years later while they were visiting Israel. There is even a documentary film entitled "Er nannte sich Hohenstein" made in our town of Podembize from photos which our mayor took of various buildings and places in 1941, he was later demoted.

7. Weihnachten Fireworks

It was Christmas Day in the year 1944, our fourth year in the designated home in what was once Poland. We alternated our celebration dinners between my parents' friends and our house. This time they, Uncle Julius and Aunt Martha as we called them, were our guests. After a delicious festive dinner and before we settled around the Christmas tree to exchange gifts, my parents and our guests decided to walk outside for some fresh air. We four girls were entertained by our personal nanny, of course.

The night sky looked unusual to the adults, instead of the bright array of stars, it was ablaze with colorful flashes in the distance somewhat in the direction of the city of Lodz about 30 kilometers away from us. Mother called out excitedly, "Oh look, they are having fireworks over there!" Father and Uncle Julius checked it and answered, "No, it's not fireworks, that must be those illuminators the Army shoots into the sky to see the bombers at night. Oh no, that must be serious!" And so the Allies were actually bombing Lodz at Christmas.

In the next week, someone knocked at our window in the middle of the night. It was one of our Polish customers who had been secretly listening to the underground radio "Free Europe". He was quite exited and told my parents that the Russians were only about a day away from our town. "Mr. Strauss, get your family and kids to the next train in the morning – to get out of here." We did, our parents dragged us out of bed in a hurry, and in the dusk mother and her four girls boarded the first train. Not surprisingly, others had gotten the same message, so there were many other families on the platform.

Unfortunately, father could not come with us, because he had received a telegram to show up at the nearest militia the same day to be drafted to the "Volkswehr" (people's reserve). If he had gone with us instead, he could have been shot for being a traitor. That's the predicament we were in. So we boarded the train to our aunt Erna's home, thinking we would be safe there. But our stay only lasted about two weeks.

* Emma on the Road (story repeated)

Back in the winter of 1945 on an icy bitter-cold January morning we found ourselves as part of a long caravan of refugees on a road in Pommern (East Germany), trying to escape from the Soviet Army which was steadily pushing ahead, while the receding Nazi Army was trying to hold them back for us civilians. Some days we were only 10 to 15 miles away from the fighting front. At night, while we slipped into an empty, cold house just to get a few naps of sleep or to find some food, we could see the red glowing horizon of burning towns or villages. How long, before the enemy will catch up with us?

One event stayed as clear in my mind as if it happened yesterday and I call it "Emma On The Road". We were all women folk on this old wagon (the men including my father had been drafted to war). The estate owner (Gutsbesitzer) of our town let people take any vehicle and horse team to escape from the oncoming Russians before he and his family took off in their own car. Our "donated" wagon was drawn by two heavyweight field horses, they were maybe 20 or 25 years old. We took only the most necessary things so as to leave enough room for 12 people: my Aunt Erna, her five children and her mother, and my mother Lola with us four daughters. Luckily, my mother was raised as a farmer's daughter and knew how to handle horses, while Aunt Erna was a city lady, her husband being the principal of the high school in town. And "Oma", the grandmother of my cousins, played the role of nanny to all of us nine children.

On that particular day, the old horses acted up, we had trouble moving on and eventually pulled over to the side, while the caravan of refugees on loaded horse-drawn wagons and people walking alongside kept passing us. Our horses were so stubborn, they just stood there and mother tried all she knew to get them going. We became more worried, should we give up our vehicle and beg other refugees to take us with them? But who would want to add twelve helpless people to their load?

All of a sudden, I heard my mother scream "Oh, Emma, Emma!" She had recognized her cousin among the by-passers, a tall young lady walking besides her folks' wagon. I can still see them in my mind, my mother and Emma hugging each other, when Mom asked, "Where is your baby?" She replied, "Oh, it died just a few days ago, we had to bury it in the snow in the ditch." As refugees, there was no time to find a cemetery or a minister, most towns were already vacated, so they made a grave by the roadside. But then Emma pulled herself away from mother and ran to catch up with her family wagon before she would loose sight of it.

My imagination completed the picture of this encounter of the two ladies, and I thought, "Maybe God had to slow us down, so we would see Emma, and so that mother could hug her and pray with her to encourage her." I was too young as an eleven year old to anticipate the miraculous encounter as an act of God and what He had to do before this scene would pass before my eyes. These two women were friends and neighbors in our homeland in Galizia (Poland), but were uprooted from their village in 1939 by the Nazis and forcefully relocated to live in different regions of the Warthegau. They hadn't seen each other for a long time.

To compound the problem, we were part of a stream of thousands of refugees traveling different uncharted routes, and we were hundreds of miles away from home. Just to run into your cousin like that is no coincidence, but a sheer act of the *God-of-the-Splitsecond*. This encounter would not have happened, if we had chosen another route or had not been delayed by lazy horses, etc. No chance for a coincidence.

8. Bullet with Your Name On It

That's what they say, when someone gets shot. But that may be a fatalist's concept of destiny. I have more problems with understanding the providence of God and the possibility of choices we make that affect our lives. Anyway, there was a moment, when I almost would have been killed, and it made me wonder, why I was not. Here is the event. On one of those nights on the road in the state of Pommern we entered a village where the people had already escaped before us. It was a desolate place. You could hear dogs barking and the mowing of hungry cattle and pigs squeaking in the barns, because there was no one to feed these deserted creatures.

We drove into the courtyard of one of these vacated farms to get some sleep. As we settled in the farmer's kitchen, my mother scrounged through the pantry and the cellar to find some food for us hungry travelers. She found some potatoes and lard or bacon, and one of us kids even discovered some freshly laid eggs in the shed. Another dinner and source of strength for us, how wonderful! The two women put the babies and the little ones to bed first. The rest of us settled on one large bed for a brief slumber.

The room was ice cold, there was no one there to heat up the room for us before we got there. So we kept our clothes on to keep warm, while the cold January wind was howling outside. At least we had some roof over our heads for a few hours. But we kept hearing the rumbling of canons in the distance. And the sky on the horizon was aglow like a sunset put on "hold", because some towns nearby were burning, reminding us that the front was frightfully near and that we must hurry on in our flight.

But we needed to comb our hair and untangle the braids which had been neglected for a couple of days. I as the oldest girl had to help braiding the little girls. All of a sudden we heard an ear-shattering "bang" and I was thrown against the wall. What happened? Here was a heavy canon bullet that had brushed my leg, raced through the heavy oak bed beside me and landed in the brick wall behind me. Obviously, my life was spared, and we marveled, why none of us in that room got killed. *God-of-the-Splitsecond* and his protection with millimeter accuracy?

9. Russian Pistol

I might as well add the third incident since I am in this somber mood. By the way, these horrific events are nothing compared to the disgusting and meaningless violence you get to watch on TV nowadays. So bear with me as I recall what happened on the refugee trail sometime in March 1945.

For me this incident remains a real sign of God's protection and grace. We had been on the road fleeing from the onrushing Soviets for weeks, while the German front was losing ground. Eventually, we had to give up on our old horse team and wagon and just run away for dear life. We took only what we could carry on our back, some blankets and pots, and we were able to get on a train westward, but that didn't last very long. A railroad bridge along the route had been destroyed by enemy troops. So we continued on foot along the country road, carrying the little children on our shoulders.

Then a man, who had an open platform truck pulled by a heavy tractor, had a generous big heart and let us jump onto his truck. I was standing because there was not room to sit down. Suddenly my younger sister pulled me by my skirt. I didn't know that I was too close to the edge and would have fallen off. We were so grateful to get a ride again, because every mile mattered. Towards the evening as the sun was setting, we entered a town and we couldn't see clearly in the encroaching darkness. The driver was the only man on the truck. The refugees were women and children (the men were drafted to the war, as I mentioned before). Someone met us and said we should turn back or hide quickly, because the Russians had encircled the area and taken command of that town. Before we could escape, some Russian soldiers approached and yelled in a language I didn't understand. I remember the horror and confusion, some women jumped off the truck and hid in the bushes.

Somehow I lost sight of my mother and my sisters and didn't know what to do. As I ran behind the truck to hide, I suddenly bumped into a Russian soldier. His heavy alcohol breath appalled me and he was pointing at me. In one hand he had a pistol and a curved dagger in the other. I was shocked, which of them will he use? Suddenly my mind was racing, "Traudi, don't LOOK scared, whatever you do, and don't scream." I remember my mother telling me not to show fear. Today I know why, a courageous victim can disarm the assailant. But as a frightened eleven-year old girl that night, the only thing I could do is pray. I closed my eyes and silently prayed a "Blitzgebet" as we say in German, "God, save me! And I will live for you!"

When I opened my eyes, I noticed that the Russian was stumbling backwards as if he was afraid of me and Î thought, "Why? I am only a helpless little girl." But then these thoughts seemed to provide the answer: "Didn't you just ask me to save you, Traudi? I just did, I am having my angel push him back away from you." Thank you, Lord! And today I would add: Thank you, *God-of-the-Splitsecond*!

I must add that mother showed up with the three children when everything quieted down and the Russians had gone back to their military post. She had been hiding from the raging enemy. And now she found me sobbing and trembling and tried to comfort me, "Now, now, we are all together again and everything is fine." Not to me it was, because I thought God had taken mother up into the clouds with my little sisters and they had gone to heaven in the rapture, while I was left behind as an orphan to go through the tribulation. Mother smiled when I told her this and added, "When I saw the Russians coming, there was no time to escape or to find you, so I told the little ones: 'Now children, be quiet and not a sound from you!' and I covered all of us with this blanket." I was amazed, but I sensed that they must have had a divine covering on top of mother's blanket.

I remember in my teens, I often wondered about that incident and the promise I made to God. Was I now bound to keep it? Maybe it had just been a foxhole prayer because I felt tempted to run away from my strict Christian home and live my life the way I pleased and enjoy the things that the world had to offer in art and culture and materialism. However, my quest for meaning and happiness in life had to undergo many different stages in my own spiritual wilderness wanderings in my latter years.

10. Lost and Found WW2 Style

Perhaps times of crises and trauma make us more sensitive to our own helplessness, and in those times our family experienced God's grace and protection in such amazing ways. I remember my mother reading to us Psalm 47 that says "God is our Refuge and our Strength, a present help in times of trouble!" We knew that this was the so-called Martin-Luther-Psalm, but we made it our own as we were dodging between the gun fires of the German/Russian war zone or when we tried to hide from the Allied bombers flying low over our heads and shooting at us civilians.

But there was another *God-of-the-Splitsecond* event that was more than a coincidence and I almost forgot to write about it. It happened in May of 1945 and how our father found us, his wife and four children, in the big confusion of refugees being scattered all over Germany.

You see, all the men were drafted into the war in the last minute, even boys from the Hitler Youth, as young as 14 years of age. Only old men and the very sick were exempt from the draft. So on or about January 5 my father received a telegram saying that he had to report on duty the next day in Lodz. Refusing to show up would be treason. That same morning mother took us children to the train station to visit Aunt Erna in Posen (Poznan), hoping it would be just for two or three weeks until it was safe for us to return to our home. Mother only packed a couple of suitcases with clothes, not realizing it would have to be enough for our long refugee journey westward. And that's the last time our father saw us until the war was over.

His journey began the next morning by foot together with a couple hundred untrained civilian men trodding along an icy road leading nowhere. Only the motorcade SS soldiers knew what would happen as they bullied them to keep marching in the bitter cold weather. No comparison to the Minute Men of New England. These men were called VOLKSWEHR (people's defense), quite a sad looking battalion. They didn't even know how to hold a rifle. The men felt like prisoners, hopeless, being marshaled by a desperate Nazi army.

I am sure, father would much rather have wanted to be with his family and guard them instead. The hopelessness and distrust was whispered from man to man in words like these, "when it's dark, let's hide in the bushes and escape." Some of them did, others were shot before they could get away. Eventually, father and another man managed to slip away in the dark and run. Where would he find his family? If you can imagine that he was somewhere in New Jersey, for instance, and his family was on the road somewhere in Pennsylvania along with thousands of refugees.

Meanwhile, we landed north of Berlin, thinking that the German capitol would be safe from the Russians. Aunt Erna had relatives in the suburb of Berlin and suggested that we all move there. Her aging Uncle Otto and Aunt Mariechen were so happy to see her and the kids, but they did not expect to get another woman and four children too. Needless to say, we slept on the floor in that tiny house. But it was wonderful to be in a clean functional home again and with loving people.

Then we heard bad news, namely that the Russians were "confiscating" anyone they could find who came from Eastern Europe, such as the Ukraine, White Russia, Poland or the Baltic Sea, in order to take them forcefully back to Russia and Siberia as their rightful subjects. Wow, that scared us, so we packed our miserly things. Aunt Erna joined us too to get away, meaning all twelve people resumed their journey. Our goal was to escape to the British Zone rather than risk deportation by the Communists. We weren't the only ones with that idea, thousands of people tried to get into the French-, British- or American zones as well. These zones couldn't possibly absorb all the refugees, so the British sent us back again. Whereto? Well, let's head for the place where we had been last – the Berlin relatives of my aunt.

Here comes the fascinating part of this story – the LOST and FOUND mystery. Back in 1945 we had no computers, no sophisticated search systems, and the country was in great upheaval. People wrote their names on search lists or cards, hoping to find their relatives through the efforts of the makeshift search agency set up by the Red Cross, I believe. My mother also filled out one of these cards indicating our names, last residence, temporary address etc. and that we are looking for our father. Volunteers all over the country spent many hours to match up these search lists by hand, and when they found a match, they would notify one of the parties by mail of the whereabouts of the family members.

So father received a notice that his wife and four children were presently in Freienhagen. Most trains and buses were no longer running, so he decided to walk and hitchhike to that place. When he inquired at a local store about the address, the man asked, "Are you sure, you have the right town? There are about a dozen of Freienhagens in Germany." The man looked at the paper and pointed to the little abbreviation i.O. after the name and said, "You want the Freienhagen near Berlin!" So father took off by foot to find the right town, but when he got there and inquired about Frau Strauss, he was told that the TWO Frau Strauss had left again with their children and nobody knew whereto. Meantime we had escaped to the British Zone of West Germany.

Father walked to the home of Uncle Otto and Aunt Mariechen and lingered on for some reason. He even discovered one of my sister's hand-knitted sweater on a branch – to him it was almost like Joseph's coat of many colors, a sign that his family actually had been at this place. He hesitated to leave and stayed one or two more days, waiting, hoping. Perhaps he was waiting for some mail to arrive that would give him a clue where they were, or perhaps they would show up? But we actually planned NOT to return because we didn't want to get shipped to Siberia, remember?

Meanwhile, we were sent back by the British Allies because they didn't want to keep us. Where should we go, all we could think of was Freienhagen. As we walked along the village road, people stopped us and said, "A Mister Strauss has come to look for his wife and children." And my cousins shouted, "Oh, that must be OUR dad," since they had the same family name. Who else would know the address of their relatives near Berlin besides their father? They weren't our relatives. We were sad, but glad for our cousins.

In the encroaching darkness, the cousins dashed off like Olympians and left us behind. They could only see a silhouette of a man coming down the road towards them, but as they got closer, they noticed that the man had a different gait, not at all like their father. "No, he must be YOUR dad," they yelled back to us. When we finally met on the road, we barely recognized the shabby, hungry looking man with a full beard. Indeed, it was our Dad.

Again, *God-of-the-Splitsecond* intercepted again to unite a family out of hundreds of thousands of transient, homeless refugees. Even making the British send us back at the right time, while delaying father to rush to the wrong town and find us just as we decided to come back. How wonderful are His ways with the Children of Men!

11. Little Boy Blue

There is another lost-and-found incident from the postwar period that amazed me, and it eventually involved my father as well. My aunt Emily had to flee from her home with her three boys by herself, because her husband was a soldier somewhere at the German warfront. Her oldest son Helmuth was about ten years old, her youngest was just a baby. They lived in another part of East Germany, so we were not together.

The oldest son became ill during the escape and had to be admitted to the nearest hospital, while my aunt lingered on with her other two boys waiting for his release. But the Russians got closer and she was told to go on with the other refugees and leave her son with the hospital and that they will take care of him. So she joined the ongoing march of people pushing towards the West, away from the Russians.

All she could do is pray for her son, whom she left behind, and trust her Heavenly Father that He will protect her sick boy. But she could not help but worry about how and when and where they would meet. Would you be less concerned if you had to disappear into no man's land with no permanent address and little faith in the ongoing chaos of war?

As days got worse, the hospital had to pack up and move to another location in the midst of gunfire. But eventually the doctors and nursing staff took off by themselves and left the patients behind. My cousin tells me, he remembers that he and other children crawled away to hide from the soldiers in empty barns and in the woods.

They banded together in little groups like the street children in Argentina. They found some clothes and learned to look out for themselves. The bravest of them would forage for food in the empty houses, and share some of this food with the weaker ones. Those raggedy, filthy kids looked like vagabonds. The police would capture those that were not fast or smart enough to get away in time.

Eventually, there were only three of them left, Helmuth, another boy and one girl. They would jump on trains and try to move along in any way possible. My cousin Helmuth lost touch with the other two kids, and as things calmed down some couple "adopted" him. He considered himself lucky to be living with these good people who gave him a very nice home. But where could his mother be with his two younger brothers? And is his soldier-father still alive? Those thoughts kept haunting him.

Here we come to the *"God-of-the-Splitsecond"* moment, as I call it. While sitting on the front porch of his foster parents' home near the railroad, he noticed in the distance two people walking on the tracks towards town. Soon he recognized that it was a woman and a man, and eventually he recognized that the woman was his mother and the man was not his dad, but he looked familiar. "Why, that's my uncle Wilhelm! What is going on here? How did these two find me in this place?"

You can imagine the joyful reunion. God did make it possible, but what is more amazing was that my father found my aunt's temporary refugee stay and that they got together.

As I am writing this story, I had to call my cousin and ask him to tell me again what happened BEFORE his mother found him, the "lost boy blue." I want to add that I borrowed the term from a famous painting of a boy wearing a blue suede suit.

Meantime, the war was over and my aunt Emily landed in the Russian occupied zone. You may remember from history, that the Allied Forces divided conquered Germany into four different zones (Russian, American, British and French). Aunt Emily was working for a farmer to earn some food to take home to her children, such as potatoes, vegetables, fruit and some bacon. Money was meaningless if you couldn't buy anything for it in the stores.

Another young woman was working alongside her and they talked about their families often. My aunt said, "I had to leave my oldest son in a hospital on the way and I have never heard from him whether he is alive or not." The other woman expressed sympathy for her grief and said, "The same thing happened to me, I was looking for my daughter too and I have just found her. She told me that she was part of a gang of kids who had no parents and were homeless." My aunt listened intently. And then the other woman asked, "What is your son's name? Let me ask my daughter if she knew him." Sure enough, the daughter said, "Yes, we ended up just being three of us, and one of the boy's name was Helmuth." But the girl did not know what happened to him eventually. Such faint hope, perhaps she knew her son, but where could he be? So the young woman suggested, that my aunt try to check out the towns nearby where her daughter had been staying before moving to this town.

And that led to the WALK ON THE RAILROAD track, but it still might not have helped, if Helmuth had not been sitting right there – watching the tracks. Or if he decided to leave. Thus Little Boy Blue turned out to be exuberant and so happy, because he was found and reunited with his mother again. *God-of-the-Splitsecond* at work?

At this point in our family life while we lived in Soviet occupied territory north of Berlin, we found an opportunity to escape during a 2-week exchange of refugees. And with my father's foresight make use of getting into West Germany, before it became life threatening due to the Iron Curtain spiked with mines, guards and fences, under extreme surveillance of the Soviets.

12. Escape to the West – Freedom

While we lived in the Russian occupied zone near Berlin, father kept a watchful eye and ear to learn what was going on. He and other refugees in town met whenever they could to console each other in their misery and scheme and daydream of better days to come. Father was even elected to be the principal of a public school set up in our post-war town. It must have been a joy to my father to be teaching and use his training as teacher, but he had to work under great difficulties. The teachers could not use any of the Nazi textbooks, so they had to glean and revise whatever they found and teach orally most of the time. Everything including notebooks was scarce, the industry had been destroyed during the war. So memorizing was important.

One day, father passed the local "Litvas-Säule", a concrete bulletin pillar about 2 feet in diameter and 6 feet tall, where notices and announcements were posted by town officials and individuals, instead of a newspaper. Among the clutter of notices, Papa discovered an inconspicuous announcement by the Soviet Regime, saying in German, that there will be a 2-week exchange of refugees between East- and West Germany. It stated the date and times when the border would be open. Some people, whose home was in the East (Soviet occupied zone) got stuck in the American-, British- or French zone. And they were now given the chance by the Allied forces to return to their home towns in the East. We learned later that many refugees who were stuck in West Germany decided to stay where they were rather than returning to their homes in the Russian zone. We now know why.

With my father's acuity, he saw this as a golden opportunity for our family to escape to the West, or any other occupied zone, if we could find a good enough reason for the Soviet controls at the border to let us through! We did, my parents had a postcard from some distant relative and used that as an excuse. But father also thought of other people. I think he was more like a "Paul Revere" in that decisive moment, because many people had not seen that public announcement. So father went around and told other refugees, "What have you got to lose? Now is your chance, let's go!" He organized several families, some of our relatives as well. But we were not going as a group, each family had to

vary its plot of explanations and go across the border sepa-
rately. They had to carry as little as possible, so that they
looked just like travelers, not escapees. Father's motto was,
"If you have freedom, you have everything. You can always
build another house somewhere."

The border gates leading to the British zone were thus
open at certain hours of the day during that two-week period
of exchange and you had to stand muster and answer questions to the Soviets. Father showed them a postcard with
an address and he said we had to visit that aunt in West
Germany, who was quite ill.

That was before the Iron Curtain went up in 1962
between East- and West Germany, fortified with plowed
minefields, high barbed wire fences and guards patrolling
with vicious dogs. All for the purpose of keeping people
within their glorified Soviet system. Each escape from there
was a nightmare and a deadly risk. Thank God, that barrier
collapsed on November 8, 1989, but not until some 40 years
later, when President Reagan defied the "Evil Empire" to
tear down that wall. Years earlier President Kennedy stood
on that scaffold facing the impregnable East and called out
"Ich bin ein Berliner!" ("ein" is pronounced like "ine") But
that was not enough of a show of strength, as I see it. One
of my German nephews who had been to the broken-down
Berlin Wall years later on that historic November 8, brought
me a piece of the rock as a keepsake.

One of the most dramatic escapes occurred in an unsched-
uled train ride, you may recall. An engineer of a routine train
asked if he could "put in some practice hours" on one of the
days he was off work. He had made detailed secret plans
for weeks to have members of his family and friends get on
that scheduled train at several different stations. No one else
knew that that "extra" train was not going to stop at the usual
stations along the way. So some other unsuspecting travelers
got on it too. The man at the observation tower noticed the

train and let it go through. As the engineer neared the end of the train tracks near the border of the Russian zone, he gave an extra push to his powerful engine, broke through the barrier with the train until they landed a few yards on the tracks in the "free world". Having rehearsed with his other escapees what to do, they immediately rushed out and ran away from the scene to hide behind bushes. It happened so fast that the border guards couldn't stop them. Voila!

13. Niedersachsen Home

Our next home was to be in the state of Niedersachsen (Anglo-Saxony) in West Germany which was under Allied control where we lived for 10 years until four family was able to start a new existence in the city of Hannover.

The first thing we noticed was that we didn't understand the dialect of the native people, although they were Germans too, but they spoke "plattdeutsch", which is a mixture of Dutch and English. One phrase will give it away, "ick hep me fallen"(meaning I have myself fallen, or I fell down). We children thought it was great fun to decipher that lingo and we learned it fast, but our parents never got into it, so they spoke "hochdeutsch" meaning the official high German. Another thing that we girls loved was walking in the wooden shoes that were made locally, so we felt like five little Dutch girls. We could trip and dance to a rhythm with these clumpy noisy clogs, what fun! It should have been made into a dance step.

Equally as amazing was the house we lived in. Since we were bona-fide refugees, who lost all their possessions in East Germany, we were entitled to live in a portion of the farmer's unused old framework building which he had been used to store grain and other things. It was a 500-year old framework structure, which saw many generations of that same family. The farmer and his family lived in a big new brick house. We enjoyed the mysterious old building. Half of it was still used as a barn, the other half was for us seven Strausses. Our kitchen was a tiny storage room with a wood stove, a long table and benches on both sides.

The central hallway, or "Diele" was something like a den. There was an inside water pump, because in the cold winter you could not go outside to fetch a pale of water. Our children's room was tiny and my three little sisters had to sleep three in one big oak bed. But I, as the oldest and a teenager, had a narrow army cot, but I felt privileged.

Living on a real farm, we were fortunate to have the farmer offer us a bit of his field to use as a vegetable garden. The only problem was that it was located at the end of the farm across the street. We had to carry water in buckets and pales about 200 yards away and we made several trips daily in order to water our plants. That made us appreciate the "fruit of our labor" in our own vegetable garden all the more.

14. The Gleaners - Bread and Apples

We lived as refugees in that 500-year old farm house, my father was unemployed while Germany was recovering from the ravages of a lost war. We were fortunate to be assigned to live on a farm, where we could help on the field and get paid in fruit, grain or vegetable, which was priceless. What good was a bag full of money, if you couldn't buy much for it? You couldn't go to a department store and pick up dresses, pants, or T-shirts. They didn't have stores in those days like Sears or Wal-Mart where you could pick up ready-made clothes. Everything was scares and expensive. If you needed a new outfit, you would do well to get some kind of cloth or fabric and sew the dress or the blouse. And you spent your winter days knitting anything that would keep you warm. Again no knitted goods available in stores. So your home became your only source of wellbeing.

Even the great Marshall Plan which the American government provided for the starving Western Europe as an economic startup project, did take a while to make an impact. I remember the time when the German currency of the Reichsmark was replaced by the Deutschmark. All those hoarded thousands of Reichsmark were worth nothing. Every person in West Germany stared with a uniform 40 DM per person, whether rich or poor.

But people were still suffering. I remember the daily influx of city dwellers from Bremen and other bombed-out cities, getting off a crowded train to walk through our village and beg farmers for some food. Instead of cash they brought their good clothes, jewelry, paintings and other valuable items, to trade-in for a pound of bacon or ham, or some potatoes for their starving families back home. Some of them even brought a fancy chair or small dresser in exchange for something to eat.

My father's creative mind thought of another way to feed his family and even hire other refugees in the village, when he was in charge of his ingenious summer business. He knew that the country roads between villages and towns were lined with apple trees, or plum- or cherry trees. And they belonged to the county authorities. So father would estimate, judging from the blossoms in spring, as to how many bushes of apples he could harvest from a certain stretch of trees along the roads. He then submitted a calculated bid, hoping he would get the deal from the authorities. Usually our father got those deals with money he saved up from the earnings of the previous apple year.

People were waiting for that employment opportunity at harvest time. And all five of us girls had to help, of course. We got our good rewards too! People had to bring their own ladders and baskets to pick. They loved to be part of a big harvest even though it was not from their own orchards. The children had great fun too. At the end of the day, the pickers would get a bushel or so besides their wages.

Even after I emigrated to Canada, that apple business was still going even after our family moved to the city of Hannover. Some people called our Dad the "Apfelbaron", an adaptation from the Strauss opera called "Der Zigeuner Baron" (the Gipsy Baron).

The farmers in town left portions of their crop of grain and potatoes on the fields, some of the rows at the edge and whatever did not get picked up by the machines. So we refugees were right behind them like Ruth in Boaz' field in Bible days. The forgotten ears of grain were precious, they made our bread eventually, when we took our gleanings to the local mill to have them ground into flour. And the leftovers in the bean- and pea fields or potato rows were our harvest as well.

Eventually father turned pharmacist along the way. He studied all the herbs which would be accepted by pharmacies and followed the strict rules for picking, labeling and packaging - another income source for us. No time to sit on your tuff and collect welfare lazily. In the evenings there was a time for talking and entertaining, although around a homemade sawdust-stove with pipes up to the ceiling and sticking out of the wall. Mom and Dad would serve humble homemade soup and goodies while chatting with their friends. No candlelight dinners for entertainment yet. Somehow we children never thought that we were less fortunate or poor with such adventurous refugee life.

Another great idea of my merchant father. He figured out that the deserted army barracks would make great "condos" for homeless people i.e. refugees. The concept or even the word "condo" had not been coined yet, but it was already in his head. He tried to win other refugees over to join in a financial venture and portion out sections of the barracks for various families as their own home. Mother could not envision it, she preferred the unique atmosphere of the old farm where we were living.

One day my father got wind that there were excellent leather boots in the army barracks for sale. Those were of a better quality than the post-war shoes available in stores. He must have scrounged up his savings again to buy 500 pairs of army boots. Mother was shocked at this risk taking. We girls had the job of sorting the mismatched boots and stacking them by size in the woodshed. People walked a path to our woodshed store. Yes, the boots got finally sold - with a profit.

15. Strauss Music and the Violin

I would be amiss in overlooking the musical aspect of our family which was inspired by our father's love for the violin that he played since his youth. But we also grew up at a time when people sang a lot as individuals, as groups or in church. There were no "vocal artists", we were all singers, perhaps whistlers or hummers or dedicated choir members. Even kids at school embellished their learning periods with songs, folk songs, patriotic songs, ballades, or rounds known as "canons". This ingenious musical talent was created from within, we didn't have radios or records and tapes to listen to. We could even make up our own tunes with our melodies.

Much to our chagrin we are immersed today with the usual background music in stores and public places to keep us sedated and content to some extent. But at the same time, we are made to listen to the repetitive moods and rhythms and the monotonous stories of the singer, while it invades our private world of thought. It would be nice to be serenaded with some beautiful music or melody once in awhile.

Our musical enthusiasm in our home came from mother's rich heritage of songs and hymns. We learned to memorize songs and often sang in "parts" as tenor or alto without an instrument. You call that a capela singing like the Mennonites do.

But our love for classical music came from our father, who as a student at Bielitz studied violin, although he had to play it left-handed due to his stiff arm that he injured as a boy. Father was so good at it that he played with a quartet at festivities, weddings, etc. He loved both the rich folk music of Slavic countries as well as ballads. We listened and hummed to his tunes from the Russian Wolga, Hungarian dances and many classical pieces. As you know, one of our great German legacy is the beautiful classical music created by masters like, Beethoven, Bach, Liszt, Schubert, even Mendelsohn and Strauss among others.

16. Bicycle - Deadly Fork in the Road

After we escaped to West Germany in 1945, we lived in that 500-year old frame house in Niedersachsen for another ten years. We girls spent our school days and teenage years in that village. I was fortunate to sign up for studies at the business school, but I had to travel six miles to the town of Sulingen on my bike in summer or winter. We didn't get picked up by a local school bus and could not afford the train or busfare. I don't know how I managed to hold onto my bike, while my face was getting covered with ice, or as I was bracing myself against strong winds. We did it somehow. Other workers made it the same way to their jobs in town, there was no other choice.

I forgot, before that daily bicycle routine to the business school, I was riding the train to the Latin school in Diepholz for an entire year. I had to get up early to catch the 6:00 am train, but I had to walk about a mile to the train station in the darkness all by myself. I had to pass a grove of tall oak trees and farm houses that looked like ghost towns, except a dog would bark here and there. I shuddered when I heard the old trees creak and groan and I imagined all kind of spooky things. I often said out loud, "Ach, lieber Herrgott!" meaning "Oh dear Lord!" No one else was around on that dark walk but me. No stalkers that we knew off back then.

Well, the bicycle ride home from the business school could have been fatal one day. I had to make a left turn at a Y-corner where two streets ran into each other at an angle. And there was a farmer with a high load of hey on his wagon obstructing my view. I thought I could make my usual turn, not realizing that there was a car behind that hey wagon with the same idea. That car would have leveled me to the ground, if I hadn't suddenly responded to a rather crazy idea. Who says there are no guardian angels or that the Holy Spirit cannot give instant commands?

All the sudden it seemed like someone was saying to me, "Ride the bike straight in front of you, quick!" But there was a narrow sidewalk and a brick wall of the house facing me. Anyway, I did that and spread my hands to grasp the brick wall and lean against it, when I heard that Volkswagen dashing past me just missing my bike. Wow! My front wheel looked like the figure eight and I guess I walked that thing all the way home the six miles. No cell phone to call Mom or Dad and have me picked up in a car. They hadn't invented those yet.

The following pages describe my emigration to Canada as the oldest daughter of our refugee family who sent me to my Canadian aunts who were living there with their families since World War I. This was the beginning of my discoveries in the New World.

17. The Ship and the Ocean – Footprints
On a sultry day in August of 1952, I was onboard of a little freighter ship, named "Beaverbrae", along with other emigrants. This one-time freighter was solely dedicated to bringing legal immigrants to Canada several times a year, sort-of an "Exodus" for Germans sponsored by the American Baptists. My father had made a wooden trunk for me and hand-painted the address of my destination Toronto, where we had relatives who immigrated to that city before

the Depression in 1926. I had just turned eighteen and was sent to Canada as the "scout" for our family who waited to follow. Within two years, I paid off my advanced fare, so that another person could come on the same boat.

I remember vividly the farewell scene at the train station in our town. It was both sad and funny, and it made me smile whenever I felt homesick for Germany. My mother and father and my 3-year old sister accompanied me on the bus to see me off at the station in the next town. We couldn't afford a taxi in those days.

As the train rolled in, we embraced each other one more time and said, "Aufwiedersehen!", but for emigrants that may mean many years later or never. I opened the window in the compartment and chatted with Papa, who gave me last minute "cheerios" and "take care of yourself" advice while running along the slowly moving train, Mama with Baby Ruth smiling and waving in the background. But suddenly mother could not conceal her pain any longer and she collapsed on the platform. I didn't realize that I caused such agony, should I have stayed at home? But then Papa turned around to pick up mother and said: "Oh Lola, you still have four children. And Traudi is not going to cannibals!"

That boat ride across the Atlantic took nine days, long days of walking on deck, hanging out with other people, waiting for the next meal and seeing nothing but water and sky. Rough for a land person, who had never been on the ocean before. One evening, I was on the back deck facing the sunset as it reflected over the serene waters. The churning turbines below created an illusion of a sunbathed golden road that glistened and gradually disappeared on the horizon.

Watching this beautiful sight, my thoughts turned to other things. What am I going to find in Canada? What is my life going to be like, whom will I marry, if ever? All these thoughts entered into my young maiden-heart. But I knew the Lord of History who had been our refuge and strength in so many different ways. So my heart prayed that personal prayer at the ocean eventide:

"Lord, when I will someday look back
on my life, on my JOURNEY,
    please let me see your footsteps,
trails of your leading even though they
    disappear and are invisible to others,
like this calm ocean tonight
    and the path it leaves.
Please let me see and know, and as my
    Captain, I ask you to steer and
Direct my path in my future,
    in a strange and new land. AMEN

As I am writing this book "*God-of-the-Splitsecond*", I can see traces of His path in the ocean of my life, some of them only visible to me, others burning in my heart that I want to share with you in this book. As you are sailing on life's ocean in the ship of your life,

May you trust the Lord of History
    The Christ of the Church
And guide you in such a personal way,
    That at the end of your own journey
You too may pray as I did:

MAY OUR LIVES
    Carry the cargo entrusted to us,
        The experiences lived, the tasks given,
            The friends cherished, the people served,
                Be to the GLORY OF GOD
                    And bring us to our
                        HEAVENLY SHORE.

18. A Laughter and A Continent Away

I can't think of any other "splitsecond" event that happened until 1953 in Toronto. I had emigrated as a young girl and was working as a daughter-au-pair in the home of a wealthy stockbroker, whom my Canadian aunt knew. I also had a beautiful room and a private bath on the 3rd floor of his 20-room house. My job was to do light housekeeping chores, like dusting, watering the flowers and checking on the "Misses" cooking. One of the things that frightened me, but I tried not to show my insecurity, was to remember what temperature the roast in the oven was set on by the lady of the house and to make sure that it wouldn't burn to a crisp. I only knew Celsius and was lost with Fahrenheit, especially since our wood stove at home functioned so well with some kindling and firewood which we kids carried into the kitchen on a daily routine.

I was also supposed to spend some time with the 80-year old grandmother and keep her company in the evenings and watch television with her. She was a tall attractive lady that dressed like Hollywood on vacation, and her fingers were covered with precious rings. To me this was an entirely new world – or planet for that matter. I lumped it all into the only concept I knew, "How worldly these people are! One doesn't need all that." And my judgment of their lifestyle was simple: they can't be real Christians. I was allowed to take evenings off and leave the house if I could manage to sneak out before the old lady noticed. On my days off I would take the bus downtown to the stores, the museums etc, and visit friends or go to the German church on Sundays.

On one of those days, I noticed a young German girl getting on the bus, whose voice sounded familiar, especially her laughter, and I wondered where I had heard that unusual laughter before. One day I took courage and spoke to her, "Excuse me, do we know each other? My name is Edeltraud Strauss." "Oh, of course" she said cheerfully, "my name is Natasha and we sat in the same school bench in Wandalenbrück." And I discovered that she was my best friend back in East Germany about ten years earlier. I did not recognize the attractive young lady, and what migrations and shuffling of peoples occurred in the meantime! Here we meet again – a decade later and a continent away. Surely, it must have been *God-of-the-Splitsecond* arranging this reunion.

19. Voice from the Past.

A similar event of finding old friends by means of a familiar voice occurred around 1966, when I visited my old Oberschule (latin school) in Diepholz, West Germany, one summer day after 20 years. The school was closed, but as I walked into the office, there was only one secretary working. I asked her for addresses of some of my classmates and she told me that the records of my year had been put into archives and it would take a few days to retrieve them. Could I come back another day? I was disappointed because I had traveled several hours to my old Alma Matter. In the adjoining office I heard a man talking on the phone. He must have finished his conversation and overheard my story, that I emigrated to Toronto and was going to fly back to Canada in a couple of days.

He came storming in and said, "Guten Tag, Sie sind doch die Edeltraud Strauss, die in meiner Klasse in der ersten Reihe sass. Nicht wahr?" (Hello, aren't you the Edeltraud who sat in the first row in my class?) I almost fainted, how could he reconstruct in the next room just who was talking to his secretary simply by analyzing my voice? I understand that the tonation of your voice never really changes, although your looks and physique do. Not only was I amazed that my voice brought back from his memory that German girl with blond braids sitting right in front of his teaching desk. If he remembered me after 20 years, does he remember his many students from his other classes as well? What a mind! So my teacher's memory gets a lot of credit for this one – and my *God-of-the-Splitsecond* must have smiled on this reunion too.

20. Toronto and TBC – Tyndale College

Coming to the great metropolis Toronto opened up a whole new world to me. It was quite a culture shock to move from a quiet cow town to a buzzing modern city with millions of people. But I loved it and had many good friends. We were even "adopted" by some families in our German church who invited us to Sunday dinners and an afternoon with their kids, so we would not feel so isolated and homesick. A wonderful brake for us "street people" from eating at counter diners and restaurants.

My aunt took me to the big historic Peoples Church on Bloor Street which was filled to capacity with hundreds of people and it even had a full circular balcony. I enjoyed the wonderful choir and the grand piano solos. The famous Dr. Oswald Smith and his son Paul were preachers. I had never seen anything like that service before.

Another highlight was the Canadian National Exhibition. One year I watched the first woman swimming through the entire frigid Lake Ontario from Niagara Falls to Toronto. I was part the large CNE crowd of onlookers and happened to be standing right where this exhausted but happy swimmer stepped out of the lake. And there were those frequent car trips of our youth group to the northern mountains to spend a great weekend up North, camping, exploring the Algonquins and the Hudson Bay. I just loved Canada.

While I was working in the office of a Christian publishing house I noticed several young people coming to work in the afternoon and I wondered how they managed to have such a short day. One of the girls told me, "Oh, we're students at the Toronto Bible College." She had to explain to me what that was and why they were there. "Oh you can enroll too. I am sure you would like it. Why not just try a semester?" Well, maybe I should, I had so many questions. In fact, I secretly was an obstinate student because I told the Lord, "If I can't find the answers to my questions there, I am finished with my faith!" I was ready to quit. I was so skeptical and unhappy, the doubting Thomas in persona. I remember some of the table discussions with other students and my arguing, debating, realizing my shaky position.

And then gradually, I must have changed inside without realizing it. I remember struggling over the vocabulary of Koine Greek study one week, as I sat in an empty classroom and rehearsed those difficult words. I grabbed a little book out of my bag by Horatius Bonar, entitled "God's Way of Holiness" just to get my mind off the subject I was studying, when a paragraph got my attention. I ended up reading half of the book. It was as if the Lord stood next to me in that empty place, saying, "Who are you running away from, yourself, or me?" It was a sacred moment in His presence. Much like the midnight scene which R.C. Sproul describes in his book "Holiness" when he was prompted to leave his dormitory and walk across the dark campus to stand in the moonlit chapel – summoned by His Lord.

Then there were people who made a tremendous impression on my life, like the missionary from China Inland Mission, Doug Percy and his African experience as well as the Rev. Elwyn Davies and the European mission of BCU who spoke at Urbana Intervarsity Conferences frequently. I admired the linguists from Wycliffe Bible Translators speaking on campus. Other famous preachers, like A.W. Tozer, Dr. William Fitch and Dr. Patterson Lee. And, of course, the famous accordionist Dixie Dean, who had just come from serving at the radio station HCJB, Quito, Ecuador. He knew the five Auca missionaries who had been killed by those savage Indians to whom they wanted to bring the Gospel (read the story in my book about Elisabeth Elliot in "Dayuma and the Aucas").

21. Dixie Dean and the Stolen Hohner

Another memorable person on campus in Toronto was the famous accordionist Dixie Dean, who had just come from serving at the international radio station HCJB Quito Equador. He knew the Auca missionaries who had been killed by those savage Indians. That event in January 1956 captured national interest and went like a shockwave throughout the Christian communities and caused many changed lives. I had entered college of TBC in the fall of that year.

I was fortunate to study accordion with the great master Dixie Dean, who had played on radio regularly, even for the British royalties. But most of all because he was a great person. He helped me to get a Hohner accordion reasonably, and I was elated because I always dreamed of owning one. One summer I worked at a retreat center together with other students and I used my "Gloria" Hohner for children's programs and played at the campfire. The night before we were to return to the city, one of the teachers stopped at the camp and offered to take some of our luggage back to the college, my accordion being one of the items. While he and his wife stopped at a motel for the night, someone stole the car. The teacher felt terrible, because the students belongings were also gone. When I heard about it, my heart sank. "Ahuh, Trudy, you would have idolized that accordion. So it was taken away from you." After two agonizing days, the police caught the thieves somewhere, and my treasure was given back to me again.

My hope to go to South America as a linguistic translator with Wycliffe was shattered by a poor health report. I was apparently unsuited for the tropics. I didn't want to go to some African place, and I certainly didn't want to go to Germany to those tough, skeptic snobs, as I thought. But that is exactly where I ended up, and I did enjoy the work there among children and young people after all.

22. Castle and Luther's Hideout Fortress

Our organization BCU rented a 500-year old castle in the hills of Hessia to be used as a camp and retreat center. The Baroness who owned this castle lived in a quaint mansion nearby. The small village nestled between wooded hills was a picture from yesteryear, a charming place for city people to visit.

We were living not far from Fulda, an ancient city which has a magnificent Roman Catholic cathedral and Jesuit monastery. On the way to Fulda you could see an ancient fortress overlooking the highway which was one of Martin Luther's hideouts. Remember, that Prince Philip of Hessia, whose castle still stands proudly overlooking Marburg, saw it as his main task to shelter and protect that brave learned Doctor of the Reformation. He said to Luther something like this, "God has called you to wield the Sword of the Word, and me to wield the Sword of Steel."

23. Youth with a Mission

After graduation from bible college, I entered missionary work with an organization that worked in Europe. My first station was a youth center in Bremen, where about 100 young people gathered in a church building. Part of our work included meetings and retreats, and about 20 young people committed themselves to visit some refugee camps and teach Bible lessons to children as well as adults. And one of our main tasks was to minister to the needs of many refugee families living in city camps. I had to organize and supply the large teaching resource center for these volunteers. The popular method at that time was using flannel-graph lessons and films.

24. Carola Geiger and MBR

Near Kassel, tucked away in the scenic mountains of Hessia, was a retreat center for women which was started by Carola Geiger who had an outstanding ministry to women, many of whom were widows whose husbands died in World War II, or young brides whose men were killed in action in the War. Rotenburg near Fulda was an oasis for many individuals and groups, perhaps as significant and similar to the retreat center of Francis Schaeffer's L'Abri in Switzerland.

One weekend, I wanted to recuperate at that retreat center "Im Kottenbach", but I did not have enough money for train fare, so I phoned my pastor in Frankfurt and asked if he'd know anyone who happened to go to the MBR. The pastor said: "Well, you are lucky because I know that so-and-so is going to the next town, you could get a ride with him. Tell him that I told you to call." That man was just about leaving, picked me up at the agreed upon corner and we chatted along the way. But I felt somewhat uncomfortable, he was a handsome man my age and very impressive. Did my pastor have a sinister trick in mind to hook me up with someone, I wondered?

When I returned, I thanked my pastor and said that I had an interesting ride with that architect. Silence of the other end of the phone, followed by his bellowing laughter. My pastor had made a mistake and gave me the wrong telephone number. His finger slipped one line down, same name, different driver, but a handsome bachelor nevertheless. How awkward I felt then.

25. Destiny Telephone Call

The time had come for me to leave the youth mission, and I did not want to make a mistake or take my commitment lightly and make a wrong choice. By the way, doing missionary work in those days was a life calling, much like becoming a nun. It wasn't getting on a plane for a two- or three weeks visit to another country to build a few things and come home again to the same life routine.

In fact, before you left for the mission field, and after tough examinations and preparations of the mission board to make sure they have the right person who claims to have a calling to the field, your church planned an official farewell and a solemn dedication. You stepped on the podium and the pastor and elders laid hands on that candidate and dedicated him or her for a life work.

When I found myself at a crossroads and could not see clear any longer in that missionary work, I was going through an agonizing time, like a nun wanting to leave the cloister? What should be my next step and my place in the future? So I made an appointment with a pastor I had known for years to talk about this concern confidentially. He was very understanding and helped me see things from another perspective. I was just about to leave his study, when the phone rang and the pastor picked up the receiver, "Yes, that is interesting, I have someone with me here who I think is just the right person." An apparent coincidence led to a most rewarding place that had just been right for me in an interim task in Bad Homburg v.d.H.

At another juncture of decisions, when my boss was elected to be principal of a seminary in Hamburg, I again asked myself: "What shall I do now?" There were several options open for me, I thought of teaching at some school or going to L'Abri in Switzerland. But I guess, the Lord had different plans for me.

My Canadian passport was expiring, having been away for five years, so I needed to make a trip to Toronto. But that affected my previous plans, which would eventually bring me to the United States with an Australian husband, who already had his sights set in the focus of his calling.

In case you might think that I was scheming, I still had that return ticket to Germany in my wallet to start teaching religious instructions in Public High Schools with the Lutheran State Church, which seemed like a great idea to me. But unbeknownst to me, a couple of months after I became engaged in Canada, I learned that there was a major shift in government policies, and religious instructions "Religionsunterricht" for Lutherans or Catholics were "nixed", no longer state-supported. Thus I would have lost my teaching job anyway. You might say, there is always another thing. But that is not the point, the point for a believer is to look for heavenly guidance to the One who has gracious providence for His own, as He also wisely rules our troublesome world.

26. Surprise Meeting in Ohio

In the summer of 1977, my preacher husband Denis and I decided to visit that lovely and industrious church in the suburbs of Columbus, Ohio, the one that had supported me as their missionary to Germany in the '60s. Denis wanted to meet those people whose "delegate" would have to live in their church community and spend a week in every family's home so that they could get to know that person better, not just as a speaker but as a live-in itinerate.

And they approached the Reverend Elwyn Davies, Director of the BCU, to find that person for Germany for them in his travels to various colleges. He was a well-known speaker and frequently spoke at Urbana Intervarsity Conferences. The Ohio people for some reason wanted a man and not a woman, a person with courage and insight to bring the gospel of hope and love to the Reformation country, now in spiritual ruins from the Nazi regime. If you remember, Francis Schaeffer had a similar burden for post-war Europe when he and his family went to Switzerland.

Whenever Rev. Davies came to Toronto, I was spiritually drawn to his unique messages, but I avoided seeing Europe as my field. I was interested in going to South America as a Wycliffe Linguistic Translator. I was choosy, no pagans in

Africa, and no snobbish, agnostic Germans either, please! And look what eventually happened both for the Ohians and for me?

So on our surprise visit to that church seventeen years later, we happened to run into a conference weekend, and guess who was the speaker? The Reverend Elwyn Davies, my much admired and valued director from BCU. And I didn't know that he was going to be there until both Denis and I were asked to come forward and say a few words to the congregation. Here, in the first row sat Rev. D. smiling at us, as I stood up at the podium with my husband wearing his black Anglican clergy suit and collar.

I felt the Lord was reminding me through that incident that He knows our beginning from our end, our "coming" and our "going". What new lesson I learned from the *God-of-the-Splitsecond* that weekend.

Part II

Purpose, Roots and Wings

*I*n this period of my life I was undergoing several major
changes, being thirty-something, I had chosen a new
career, that of teacher in religious instructions with the
Lutheran State church in Germany. However, having
to renew my Canadian citizenship I had to visit Canada
briefly, at which time several unexpected things happened
that changed the course of my plans.

Enter another sojourner on a ship from Australia to
follow his calling and vision, whom I met while visiting
in Toronto. And so you can read in this section about our
encounter, our studies and ministry in Dixieland as well as
in Connecticut.

Then the most dramatic experience of the Lord's
healing my husband on his deathbed to raise him up again,
as you can read in "St. Raphael's - Angel at the Bedside".

Here also I am telling of several "God-of-the-
Splitsecond" events in my widow years that followed.

27. Provocative Doorkeeper

In October of 1966, I decided to make a trip to Toronto for a visit before I would venture out on the teaching offer which I received from the Lutheran State Church in Germany as religious instructor for high school kids. Another reason was that my Canadian passport was expiring soon and I needed to renew it after being five years overseas, or I would end up as a woman without a country.

Toronto was in a festive mood, preparing for the first Canadian Centennial in 1967 and there were so many things going on. I discovered an interesting group at Knox Presbyterian Church on the edge of the university campus which met Sunday nights after the evening service. The group was called "25 to 35". That was not the size of the room but defined the age of singles and students meeting there from all over the city.

Sometimes I noticed a young man coming in late and sitting down in the back. He was dressed in a black clerical garb and I thought, "Why does this Catholic come here?" One evening as I was just about to leave for the subway and approached the heavy front door of the church hall, somebody dashed out from behind to open that portal for me. It was that priest and he said, "It was a provocative evening, wasn't it?" looking at me and smiling politely. I was so dumbfounded at the sudden chivalry but also at the unusual attention-getter, come to think of it, was it provocative, why, how? I think I mumbled something like, "Oh, I guess so." Then he said, "Are you going to the subway?" "Yes," I replied, and he added, "May I walk down with you?" And this was the beginning of our Morrow-story, or shall we say, our walking and working together for years to come.

Before I stepped on the subway, he invited me to join him for a breakfast meeting on the next Saturday at an Anglican church in Scarborough. And I don't know why I accepted, I guess it sounded religious enough not to be threatening, but it turned out to be a nightmare or rather a blizzard of an event. Let me tell you why.

I had not listened to the weather forecast and was unaware of the blizzard warning. I ended up being the only passenger on my bus. Meanwhile, my new friend's bus was cancelled, but there was no way to let me know, while I was waiting for him at the destination. Cell phones had not been invented yet. Standing at the roadside near the driveway of the church and waiting for Denis, cars kept slowing down and drivers looking puzzled at that freezing young lady, asking, "Can we help you?" All of them were black-clad clergy. I felt so awkward standing there. Eventually the same bus driver turned around, stopped and made me get into his bus. He feared that I might freeze to death in that blizzard and I took his sound advice.

Denis kept phoning my sister's home during that time to find out what had happened to me, no one knew my desperate predicament. After four hours I eventually reached home, shivering and frozen to the bone. Another phone call from Denis to apologize and console me. He invited me to see a film that evening at his college, called "A Man for All Seasons" on the life of Thomas Moore of England.

So we kept dating each other since that chilly misguided blizzard date in January. Denis was in his final year at Wycliffe Anglican College on the University of Toronto campus. I didn't know until later, that he had made a promise to the Lord, not to get involved with "another woman" again, until he was finished with his studies, after his fiance in Australia wrote him a letter while he was studying at Oxford, England, saying she was going to marry another man.

He had to deal with this great heartache and disappointment, but he remained true to his calling to the ministry and wasn't going to be broken or distracted. So he told me (much later) that his prayer was like this: "Lord, when I am going to be finished with seminary, ready for the pastorate, will you have the woman of your choice ready for me?"

Enter the scene of his last semester: a young tourist from Germany whose name is Edeltraud. I remember, during our first few coffee dates, Denis with a mysterious, mischievous look on his face would ask me, "Trudy, when is YOUR BOAT, I mean, when is your PLANE supposed to fly back to Germany?" I had a return air ticket in my pocket to resume teaching. I didn't know that in the back of his mind was the thought, "Lord, let me make sure that she is the ONE you have sent - and then I won't let her fly back."

28. Bring the Cloak and the Parchments

This is a continuation of the "blizzard date" story and the coffee shop dates. While I enlisted at the English Literature evening program at UofT as my first effort to get more credits towards my Bachelors degree, Denis would figure out how to "accidentally" run into me on campus, when I was through classes, or he would hide behind the hallmark of the university, the "Tower", much like the Harkness Tower is the Yale symbol, and he would holler "booh" just to scare me.

The Wycliffe campus was something else. I had never seen mortals in cap-and-gown running from classroom to classroom. Well, those Anglicans did and it reminded me of the University of Heidelberg or those ancient halls of learning in Europe. Why were they such traditionalists? Maybe to get used to the black clerical garb which they would wear as ministers or priests anyway?

The most dramatic event in my courtship with that Anglican was to be invited to his graduation ceremonies. What a long procession with fanfare, trumpets, acolytes, choirs, and professors in their dignified robes! Then another surprise, instead of just walking past the presenters and grabbing your diploma to run off stage in triumph, each graduate had to appear before the Chancellor, kneel down reverently while the dignitary laid hands on him and prayed and then gave him the graduation scroll.

It was the beginning of my marvel at the ritual and traditions of the Established Church. Has this young lutheran-baptist lady gone berserk and would Martin Luther denounce her apostasy? Not really, because I was in love with a traditionalist, whose essence was a much deeper personal faith and walk with his "ever present Lord of History" than was mine anyhow.

Oh, I forgot to tell you about the books and parchments. After that impressive graduation ceremony, it was time for my friend to look into pastoral openings. He had been making contacts during his last year at college anyway. One day he proposed to me with the hidden agenda, "How do you like cold weather?" He had apparently received an offer to take on a small church in Alaska. I soon realized that if I was to share my life with him, I would have to accept his vision and dream for his life before anything else I had in mind. But I shuddered at the thought of being frozen in some arctic town, although as a European I really enjoyed white winters.

Eventually an offer of pastoral work and teaching at a parochial school in New Haven, Connecticut, came up. Denis said, "That is the most European city I can think of where you will feel at home." He probably meant the Gothic architecture of Yale University. So we did move there, and I got a new man, a new country, a new home - and NEW ENGLAND too.

BOOKS, BOOKS, I must tell you about them. The offer for Denis to teach in New Haven in the fall of 1967 came so sudden that he had no time to pack his belongings which were permanently kept in the attic of Wycliffe, since he was a foreign student, an Australian, who had no relatives in Canada. We became engaged and made a celebration trip to Montreal to see the Canadian Centennial Exhibition in August - what fun we had at the EXPO 1967. I even got to touch one of the remaining Gutenberg Presses and we got a copy of the first printout. Who cares, certainly not our youngsters who might never hold a book in their hands had it not been for the invention of the 42 line typeset?!

But the teaching job for Denis at St. Thomas in New Haven was about to start in two weeks. So I got the job of packing and shipping his array of books and other belongings he left at the college. As I rummaged through the stuff and read the titles, I came to know him better. "Mmh, that man has this book too?" I mumbled and read his notations on the margins.

My own emigration to the USA could have taken a year and would have ruined our wedding plans, but the immigration officer discovered the word "Poland" in my passport and said, "Oh, Miss Strauss, you could get there in two months as a Polish person." "But I am German" I replied. The entire USA quota for Poles was only 100 persons per year! And not even that many could make it through the tight Iron Curtain of the Soviets in Poland. So I landed in New Haven at Christmas.

29. Morrow & Morrow & Morrow.

Scene: Airport in Toronto, Friday, March 15, 1968, one day before our wedding was to take place in Buffalo, New York. I had just disembarked from the plane from New York City and had to go through Customs to enter Canada properly. I was to stay overnight with my sister's family, who even planned a surprise bridal shower for me for that the evening.

Here I was in the passenger line, dragging my suitcases with enough clothes for the honeymoon and, of course, the self-made wedding gown, etc. I kept worrying, "Have I not forgotten anything?" and my thoughts were preoccupied with tomorrow's agenda. "Will Denis make it in time for the plane to Buffalo?" He was expected to meet us at a little Episcopal church in time for the wedding ceremony. And those arrangements were made by mail and telephone, because he had not yet received his permanent US visa in time for the wedding in Toronto, so our family and friends had to travel to Buffalo USA this side of the Canadian border.

While I was preoccupied with my own thoughts, I heard the customs-officer call out: "Morrow?" and I jumped forward, but I wondered why he had called me instead of the man in front of me. The officer looked at me surprised, "Is your name Morrow?" "Well, yes," I answered, "<u>Oh no, it will be Morrow tomorrow</u>," I mumbled as I realized there was some confusion but also a strange coincidence, because the passenger standing in front of me was a real Morrow by name. I didn't realize that the officer had been reading that name off the passport he held in his hand.

To add to this unusual event, a longtime friend of mine whose name was also Morrow, was waiting for me at the airport. He was going to take the role of the bride's father at the wedding, since my own parents were not able to come from Germany.

And the third surprising element in this incident was a secret, that we all learned about at the wedding reception. The pretend-father of the bride raised his champagne glass and stated emphatically, "I would like to toast TWO brides and not just one, the lovely NEW Mrs. Morrow!" and he continued, "My toast is also to another lady, Mary, the lovely bride whom I married many years ago on this same day!"

You can imagine our applaud was doubled for this unusual toast.

Thus, we have a Morrow & Morrow & Morrow event. I don't know why it happened like that, but I think that *God-of-the-Splitsecond* must have a sense of humor. It certainly amused us.

Our honeymoon was rather taken by installments because we just moved to New Haven and did not have enough vacation days or money, for that matter. This way we had inadvertently stretched our lovely experiences in the country of our choice over several months. Denis had two positions, as a seminary graduate he was ministering to the youth group of a large Episcopal Church and was also teacher at a private school which the church sponsored on its premises. One of his boys exclaimed in his science class one day, "I hate molecules!" That same boy turned out to become a significant scientist lateron.

30. Quincy and John Adam's Cow Pasture

After my husband's teacher/ministry years in New Haven, we moved to Boston where he continued his postgraduate studies. He received a Master of Theology at ENC and a Master of Divinity degree from the Episcopal Divinity School in Cambridge near the Harvard campus.

One of our rented apartments was in Quincy, Massachussets, and incidentally quite close to the "Adams Saltbox", an old landmark house under historic protection. We learned from a neighbor that the place we lived in was once John Adam's cow pasture. And next to the Saltbox was now MacDonald's Restaurant. Well, on Saturday mornings Denis would usually say, "Come, let's jump over the fence." We did, just to make a shortcut for some piping hot coffee at MacDonald's. Mr. Adam's cattle were no longer in sight - we were!

Another historic feature of Quincy was the new home of the Adams family and his son John Quincy Adams. It had an impressive famous library, a separate stone building consisting of one large paneled hallway surrounded with quaint balconies along the four walls with winding stairs leading to the main floor. This preserved library is filled with thousands of books. Ever wonder about our "uneducated" Puritan forefathers? They didn't waste their time on TV education with hours of stupid, mind-numbing advertisements either. How we have been robbed of our time to think and learn. Will the latest cyberspace be the final breakthrough or an uncharted information jungle? What is going to happen to those tomes of unchanging wisdom contained in many a good book - to become extinct? Since writing this book in 2002, we have inherited another plague, the cell phone, although it is a vital communicator, the noise in the ear in many shuts out any other.

Well, that John Adam's Estate is kept as a tourist place and is meticulously maintained in its originality. From the subway window you might see a man tending to his farming chores on a wagon pulled by oxen and other servants in original attire taking care of the premises. However in the springtime, the hill is ablaze with a field of DAFFODILS and crocuses gleaming in the sun. One can see that colorful splendor from the Cambridge-Dorchester subway, and people flock to that side of the train just to look and say "Oh, Oh!" I wonder why the train hasn't toppled over yet from the sheer weight of people shifting to the other side. But when I pass that Estate, I can't help but think of John Adam's wife ABIGAIL, perhaps walking from house to library with her children or to oversee her many chores at home, while her husband JOHN was perspiring in that hot July Assembly hall in 1776 in Philadelphia during those birthpang weeks of the DECLARATION OF INDEPENDENCE. It was from this daffodil-covered hill that Abigail wrote her famous "DEAR JOHN!" Letters. There were no telephones yet.

31. Boston and the Harvard Campus

Boston became our student home for the next three years, while my husband did his post-graduate work. He had a tight schedule, attending classes during the day, sleep during afternoon and then off to a night job and get ready for college in the morning. I worked during the day and studied in segments in the evenings to get my bachelors degree. We liked Boston, it is a rather unique cosmopolitan city with a small college town flavor. A charming little metropolis, where you can easily get from one end to the other in a brief car ride or subway, not like the endless jungle of New York City, a county to itself with 15 million people. We enjoyed many things, among others, the concerts with Arthur Fiedler and his orchestra at the banks of the Charles River. We relived history and enjoyed the atmosphere in Boston.

We loved to go to Park Street Church, it was such an interesting and lively congregation and had a large group of Harvard students and many visitors. The pulpit was occupied by many a famous preacher, located on the corner of Beacon Hill near the Capitol and the Commons, where the Puritan settlers used to have a common grazing ground.

One Sunday we visited the church across the street, called Tremont Temple. Sitting in the last row of a packed audience, I pinched my husband hard in the arm. Imagine, here was my favorite minister from my student days in Toronto of about 20 years ago. What a surprise! Looking back, I must say that many things were not coincidental, but arranged and transformed through the loving hand of our Lord. The next story is one of those.

32. Pow-Wow with the Indians

One day in 1973 we walked into a crowd surrounding a media setup. It was supposed to be a TV newscast on the plight of the Indians who had lost their land to the Americans many years ago. Some Indians, dressed up in their native costumes and warrior outfits, just finished their makeup for the show. "This is interesting to see real Indians" Trudy thought.

But when a camera man held the microphone to her for a comment, she raised the question, "How about my land in Eastern Europe, which my ancestors claimed as original settlers some 200 years ago? They claimed virgin woodland from bears and wolves and cultivated it into choice farmland. They paid for that land and became subjects in the Austrian-Hungarian Empire. The Poles took it after World War I, the Nazis took it in 1939 and deported us to Germany. The Russians finally took it in 1945 and we never got it back. Four government changes in one lifetime. So my question is: Whose land is it really? How come that WE as the original settlers of that land didn't get it back? The media-man didn't want to tackle that one. Some politically correct guys, who didn't want to take on the "Evil Empire"? And they quickly turned to another bystander for more questions.

Postscript 2002: Even in 1989 when Soviet Communism collapsed and the Berlin Wall, that infamous Iron Curtain, fell and Germany became united, only 1/3 of the German territory was returned, and our Galizia communities were handed over to the Ukraines under the Soviet Union. Few people realize that today. My husband never heard that bit of news about the collapse of Communism, he had already passed away in 1982.

33. On the Subway in Hamburg.

If you know that Hamburg has about two million people, you can imagine what the subway looks like at rush hour, something like London or New York. Well, try to meet or find someone. You have to select a certain spot or landmark where you would wait for your friend.

Denis and I were visiting different places in Germany in 1973. We took a cruise along the wide Elbe River and saw the many harbors of this famous city. I was hoping to find a girlfriend in Hamburg with whom I worked for years, but whose address I had lost. I tried everything to locate her, contacted the town hall, her friends, but nobody knew her whereabouts. So I gave up hope of finding her in Hamburg. After a long city tour and harbor cruise, we were heading for the right platform to catch a train to my parents' home in Hannover. But we were moving against the stream of commuters on their way home from work.

Suddenly I screamed "Brunhilde" and my husband gave me a puzzled look, then he smiled and pointed to the ceiling – and I knew what he meant. He stepped back, while we embraced each other and I said, "How wonderful to see you here, I have lost your address and tried everything to find you." And Brunhilde said cheerfully, "How amazing to meet you here in the subway, I was just on my way home from the office." And the rest is history.

That was another *God-of-the-Splitsecond* event. If we would have stopped at a restaurant for some food, or taken a different staircase, or arrived at the subway an hour later, we would have missed her. It was more than a coincidence. It was God arranging a few things to make this happen. But what we little finite beings don't realize is that we only see the working out of it and reflect on "our decisions". We don't know what goes on in the heavenly planning scene beforehand. How much we need to rely on His guidance and be open to His will.

34. Rebecca at the Well.

I am sure, you are familiar with this story in Genesis Chapter 24, where the old patriarch Abraham sends his servant to his homeland of Mesopotamia to find a bride for his son Isaac. That story could be more an answer to prayer of a preordained encounter. Or it could be a fleece which the servant put out to make sure that he would recognize the person he was supposed to meet?

I have often wondered, what would have happened if another girl had showed up as the first one at the well, one that wouldn't have been willing to give the camels water as well. It is obvious that the "other" girls got distracted or delayed on their errand. I am fascinated about how the events fall into place, both for the servant and for Rebecca, a sign of the wisdom of *God-of-the-Splitsecond*. Some reader might get the impression that I believe in fatalism, instead there are plenty of chances to make choices and use our free will.

And this story is recorded in the Scriptures for the encouragement of our faith. It is such a beautiful love story and shows what a wonderful faith these people had, not only in the goodness of their kin (relatives) who also knew the Lord Jehovah, but they also trusted the character of the stranger with a mission to invite him into their home. How pathetic such a venture would look today, there would be agents and detectives (and the internet) scurrying to get the most out of this situation or to prevent a wrongful match?

35. On the Steps in Philadelphia.

In the spring of 1976, my husband and I attended an Episcopal Conference in Philadelphia. At that time he was the minister of a parish on the Delmarva Peninsula. In case you don't recognize the name, it stands for what was once a tri-state effort to rename the Eastern Shore, and is made up of <u>De</u>laware, <u>Mary</u>land and <u>Virgini</u>a.

We were interested in the new "PewsAction" gathering and enjoyed a bit of sightseeing. On one of those high stone steps leading into a church, we ran into a couple that we knew about eight years ago in our student days in New Haven.

After a brief exchange of happenings etc, the man asked, "Would you be interested in a pastoral change? Can I put your name on our candidate list?" Denis was surprised to receive this offer, especially since there are different regions for vacancy listings and New England was not in our area. We also learned that the candidate list had already been closed. But now it was reopened, and eventually Denis was unanimously voted in by the committee to come to New England.

While we were roaming the streets of Philadelphia, not like that film star Stallone in his lonely search for meaning, we found ourselves in an apparent coincidence which again must have been guided by *God-of-the-Splitsecond*.

36. Dangerous Magnolia Tree

Our first parish was near Salisbury, Maryland, on the Delmarva Peninsula, which is surrounded by the Chesapeake Bay on the south, the Atlantic on the east, and the Hudson River on the north. The peninsula is laced with marshes and wetlands, rivers and bays for boating and sailing. It still maintained much of the charm of the old Dixieland, rich farmland for corn, soya beans, watermelons, peaches, to name a few. You can also see large franchise Chicken-Perdue farms and large flocks of Canada Geese resorting in the fields, and tourists from Washington and Philadelphia or New York.

Spring Hill Parish was actually made up of two separate Episcopal churches to share one minister or priest, but they were different in nature like town and country. They were friendly, hardworking, solid families who treasured their rich history and the legacy of previous generations dating back to George Washington's days. But most of all, their real personal faith in the Lord made them special to us.

It was quite a change for both of us to come from large impersonal cities to a little community that you could count by the number of main-street lights. When we walked along the road, we could stop and visit part of the congregation right then. One Sunday, we were invited by the Black Community Church to join in their service. It lasted for about three hours, what a happy time they had. They were still carrying on after we left the service.

But there is more to our time at Spring Hill Parish. I only want to mention one event, which ties in with my *God-of-the-Splitsecond* idea. When one of our parishioners died at the age of 90, the family asked my husband to come to the house and he took me along. While the minister and the widow and her daughter were conversing with each other in that sorrowful moment (me, the quiet observer sitting nearby), a gray-haired old black man, an Afro-American, comes into the living room, hat in hand, goes to the old widow, kneels down and buries his head in her lap and sobs: "Oh Massa, Massa, he was such a good man!"

Now was this necessary, I ask you, after all those years since the Civil War and the Civil Rights Movement of the 60s? Indeed not, but here was evidence of a truly amiable Christian relationship that had been going on for years, for generations, on this very plantation since the landing of the British. That old black man was the Chief of the entire large farm, the boss, not a slave, who himself was born on this "plantation." He owned a beautiful house, a luxury car, many conveniences, and everything he needed, so did others of his race in our town, as I learned. I shall never forget that scene with "Massa", sorry, not to be found in today's textbooks.

One day, when making house calls with Denis, I stayed outside to admire the beautiful landscaping and that spacious magnolia-tree lined driveway of that estate. I was fascinated by that gigantic old tree draping like a giant mushroom over the lawn. I was tempted to duck underneath the drooping limb and branch of the magnolia canopy just to see what it looked like, when the lady of the house appeared at the front door, saying goodbye to my husband on the front steps.

She noticed me at the magnolia and hollered over to me, "Trudy, watch out, don't go there, there might be a snake!" If she would not have warned me right then, I might have been an unsuspecting victim. For lo, as I looked up to the arching branches above me, I saw a snake wrapped around one of these thick limbs, perfectly camouflaged. But now my eyes - and my heart pounding with fright, spotted that snake. I didn't dare to answer the lady, "Oh yes, I see a snake sitting right there." Instead, I moved quietly out from under the tree walking backwards and not letting that snake get out of my sight. You can imagine that I thanked my Lord for His deliverance and for being "a very present help in trouble" (from Psalm 46.1)

One of my favorite songs is *"In that Great Kingdom Morning, Fare Thee Well, Fare Thee Well"* or the song *"Swing Low, Sweet Chariot"*. These songs were once called Negro-Spirituals, now they are dubbed Gospel Songs. But they do not mean the same thing. It has a special meaning to us who remember history. To call it "Gospel" is just like saying, "I like classical music" without specifying what in particular, which composer, what type, what setting (Baroque, Symphony, Verdi, Bizet, Bach or the Beatles or the Blues for that matter). So if you say "Gospel Music" it could be anything from the English Methodists hymns to Appalachian music to Western style - with religious content, and you have lost the focus and the uniqueness.

To me, Negro-Spirituals bring out the deepest sympathy and the greatest admiration of those believers who had gone through great suffering. They were great people of faith and have made a great contribution to the American

Dream. People in the image of God who longed for freedom like any other human. That's why today I can get carried away and I join them in exuberant song like the Brooklyn Tabernacle Choir and others. It is just as wrong to celebrate Johann Sebastian Bach without the reason and the setting, why he wrote that music which was an expression of his faith and his love for Jesus. He even signed each piece "In Jesu Namen" IJN or in Latin SDG (sole deo gloria).

When I was a child, mother read to me from the book of Harriet Beecher Stowe, "Uncle Tom's Cabin" in German text. We were then under Nazi dictatorship. I learned to see that there were other people in the world suffering for their faith. Amazing, that little women who wrote that book lived in the hills of North Guilford nearby.

37. Connecticut Parish

A little white Episcopal church on a hill facing the Northford shopping center was our second parish. We moved up to Connecticut from Maryland on a sunny day in July of 1976. As you know, it was the Bicentennial Year marking 200 years of United States history.

Just a few days earlier on the 4th of July, we saw hundreds of tall ships and schooners from different countries sailing down the mighty Chesapeake Bay in this glorious celebration of 1776. It looked like a peaceful Armada of Spain of yesteryear. These "Tall Ships" were on their way to New York City and the Hudson River and passed the Liberty Statute to commemorate this spectacle.

Their immense sails unfolded gleaming in the sun. Other ships had their sails all neatly rolled up, like the "George Focke" of Germany, with dozens of her sailors in white uniforms standing on those beams - like birds on a telephone wire. While we were watching with the crowd, I could not help but think. What would have happened, if America had not taken the course charted out for her by the Founding

Fathers in that amazing document called the "Constitution"? What would have happened, if the Bill of Rights, penned by those wise, godly men, had been written by the Troika, or the KGB, or even the SS of Germany? Would these ships have come from many countries to help us celebrate 200 years of history today? Would there be anything left to celebrate?

Meantime, our belongings were lovingly being carried off in a moving van by helpful members of our new parish. Some of the men of our parish came even to help us pack all our stuff in Maryland. My husband had a large library, four walls of his study were covered with books, my own small collection blending with his extensive history, pastoral and educational sets. So there were about 60 boxes of his library at least. Wow! In addition, I had acquired a collection of arts and crafts material in Boston and in Quantico. I was lucky to have my own craft-loft or studio above our garage, and I was into creative stitchery and fiber sculpture, you see. Some of our young people came to try their thing in this workshop too.

Why am I mentioning all this? Because all these boxes stored in the basement of our new Connecticut parish house for later unhurried unpacking and arrangement became part of a flood emergency trap, for me at least. About three weeks later, a major downpour flooded the basement - and there were the boxes! We were warned on the radio, but how to move or raise all those boxes in a hurry? There was no other way but for me to carry most of these upstairs in one afternoon (the books). I never had such awful muscle pain since. Apparently all this volunteer help was undone in one rainy day. And frankly, I didn't have the nerve to call anyone to help me move this stuff after they had just displayed their helpfulness in our recent move. And my husband was not at home, making house calls on our parishioners. No, we didn't have cell phones as yet.

38. Mary's Christmas Pageants

St. Andrews was blessed with some very dedicated people, who put in so much time and energy for the work of the church. Among these was an old couple, Dr. Leslie Hotson, a famous Shakespeare sleuth and his wife Mary, both now in their mid-eighties, who worked with the children for about 25 years to put on a special Christmas Pageant, written and orchestrated by Mary. They had no children of their own, but instead many "children of the heart". I can't help but think of the Passion Plays in Oberammergau, where the father who was "Peter", taught his son to take on the same role and they had to memorize the entire text. So here we had generations of pageant-kids and a wonderful long tradition of getting children involved in the Nativity. By now there were 25 Marys of the pageant at our church.

One thing Mary missed was real candles in the tall church windows at St. Andrews. She said, "we used to have those real candles in the windows every year, and the church did not burn down." One year, we surprised her and had electric candles placed in the windows just for the pageant. Did you know that the Pilgrims and the first settlers put a candle in the window at Christmastime to signify Christ being the Light of the World? Another meaning, that this home was to be a shining light and a welcoming sign for a wayfaring stranger.

39. Blanket for Baby Jesus

One of my church school children, a little redhead girl with so much wit and deep feelings, came up to me one Sunday morning and said, "Mrs. Morrow, the Christchild in the manger is soo cold! Could we put a blanket over it to keep it warm?" At first, I thought she meant our own manger scene inside our church, because she herself was our Mary in the pageant that year. "No, I mean the Baby in the Manger at the TOWN SCQUARE."

You see, every year we had a beautiful big Nativity Scene in our town with life size figurines, Mary and Joseph and the Shepherds and animals, inside a carpentered stable at the busiest intersection of our town, at the old Triangle Green corner of Rte. 22 and Rte. 17.

Well, I can't hurt a little girl's feelings, I thought, so I suggested to her, "Tell you what, we'll find a blanket in my house and we'll both walk over to the Green and cover Baby Jesus." We did just that, but it was such a touching moment for me, I couldn't help but be reminded of the "LITTLE DRUMMER BOY", one of my favorite Christmas carols. We need drummer girls as well, now more than ever. And meantime, the ACLU has intimidated us into removing the Manger, the real witness of Christmas from our town square.

Was anybody else out there concerned enough about the Christchild to protect it from the onslaught of radicals and prevent them from removing this essential reminder of Christmas? Did anybody care enough for the children, so that they could see and touch and maybe show their devotion to Jesus? We can spiritualize all we want, children need concrete reminders. Sadly, now we sing "Away FROM the Manger", while the essence of this Season has been replaced by Santa Claus and Snowmen.

Christmas Day 1979 was the 25th year of the Pageant and we had a special service, when 14 of the 25 "Marys" gathered at the altar for dedication. At one of the children's rehearsals of the children, Mary Hotson said, "Now imagine twenty generations of Marys back and you would find the Christchild in the manger in Bethlehem." How simple and picturesque to look at the time span of centuries like that.

On that retirement pageant in our church, Mary requested that she and myself walk up to the altar with the communnion elements of wine and bread. It seemed to me like two childless Marys of the Church, herself as the pageant creator, and me, as the Mother of the Church School children. It was a touching experience of farewell, also for both of us, since it was my husband's last service at St. Andrews.

40. Cosmos and Christmas

Since Mary's Pageant was presented in the sanctuary every year using the nave and the center isle, I planned a Nativity program for the rest of the Sunday School with all of the children involved in it and I used the parish hall for that program. One year, I was energized by Carl Sagan's controversial "Cosmos" TV program, where the entire human history is squeezed into the last few minutes of December 31. You may recall Sagan standing on a huge calendar of the month, all of it representing billions of years of evolution and he depicted the period of humans as the last "millisecond" of the universe!? According to his philosophy humans are a tiny segment, maybe even an afterthought, as "whoever or whatever" was working on a trial and error basis. Somebody said, it takes more faith to believe in chance than in creation considering the odds.

Being challenged by Sagan's miniscule humanity, I went into a large-scale Christmas story myself and involved the universe in a different way, starting with an imaginary conference meeting of the Archangels. Lucifer appearing late and arrogant, bringing the great news that God was about to create a planet he called Earth, etc. I wove the Fall of Lucifer into the drama, who eventually dragged one third of all the angels with him in his exodus. That took care of most of our angelic kids, who followed the rebel angel down the isle of the church. All those wayward angels would later appear on stage again as shepherds and Israelites.

Then Archangel Michael, taking leadership in the redemption story and giving the little children a chance for their traditional "Away in a Manger" song inside a huge wooden boat depicting the Ark, here the ark of the church. A couple of years later I reenacted the drama in the large sanctuary of Christ Episcopal Church in Guilford, which was the ideal setting for that pageant, using the elaborate Altar section, the sanctuary and the nave for it. We had a dramatic backdrop panorama of stars above the Altar with moons and comets suspended from the tall Altar ceiling and the stage was illuminated by tiny lights dangling from the ceiling. It was quite an unusual Christmas scene. The church was filled with parents and friends, and the kids were getting ready for the pageant in the dressing room. Just minutes before the kids were to enter on stage from the choir loft, I peeked in to see if everything was alright, and I couldn't believe my eyes.

One of the younger girls went on stage by herself and placed the little cradle with the Christchild (a doll) below the stars. She must have discovered the little cradle in the dressing room. But that was not in my original script. The COSMOS was supposed to be the center of the pageant. Should I go quickly and remove the cradle? What would the parents and visitors think. Would I hurt someone's feelings - or even appear like the ACLU (the secular Grinch in America) who is removing the manger from the Christmas scene in public places? "No, better leave it," I thought. And I cannot forget the unscripted sneaked-in Christchild in the manger. I guess, it must have been a traditionalist, who did this.

Would you know, that funny, unplanned little deviation was the thing that people remembered most, because when you looked at the stage from the audience, you saw - no, you experienced - a strange awesome feeling. That vast universe of stars and constellations and the wee little Christchild in the basket holding up its hands into the sky, saying:

Yes, I made all this, I am the Creator and Upholder
and Redeemer of this. This is why I came at Christmas,
for the lost part of my Universe.
I CAME FOR YOU.

Among the audience was my husband in a wheelchair, who had special permission from the nursing home to come that evening. Denis became ill with encephalitis a few months earlier and was partially paralyzed. He liked our pageant and the unusual manger being the ARK of Noah, which was to represent the Church in a turbulent world. It was a huge cardboard boat, in which the little children were standing, singing "Away in a Manger." But as a thoughtful theologian, my husband added "Trudy, did you think of the ARK of the COVENANT? You know, the priests had to carry that Ark and look after it."

41. St. Raphael's - Angel at the Bedside.

In July of 1980, my husband, age 50, suddenly became ill with encephalitis and was in a coma for weeks. His case was the most serious one and it made it twice to the Physicians' Conference at St. Raphael's. They initially suspected that he might have caught Limes Disease, of which the first victims showed up that same weekend.

It was strange for me to talk to a man who did not respond in his coma, so I decided to sing hymns and melodies quietly or read from the Bible, hoping he could hear. One day, a young nurse peeked into the room and said, "Oh, do you love Jesus too?" seeing me holding the Bible at his bedside. As the nurse entered the room, she said quietly, "I come to this hospital from Hartford once a week for training and I ask the Lord where I should go and he seemed to say "West, the 4th Floor". Oh well, one of those Charismatics, I thought. But anyhow it was an unusual encouragement to me in my lonely condition. Was it another *God-of-the-Splitsecond* moment?

Every night I drove from the office to St. Raphael's Hospital, stopping to grab a quick meal at MacDonald's drive-in and spend the evening with my husband. This was my routine for about three weeks. One day I drove home instead to pick up something before going to the nursing home. As I entered our apartment I had an eerie feeling, it seemed as if there was an oppressive presence there and I had never experienced anything like it before. I was even afraid to stay in the house. And I thought, "Shall I go for a ride or head for the mall? No, I'd better go to a prayer meeting, but where is there one tonight?" The only place I could think of was Grace Church in Old Saybrook, a place where my husband visited often. There was quite a crowd present in the meeting, but none of them I knew. The leader asked that we share prayer requests, so I reluctantly expressed mine. But I remember adding, "my husband is in a coma at the hospital. Please pray for his life, but not because he is my husband. Other women loose their husbands too, why should I be different? Pray for the life of a minister, whom, I believe, the devil would like to wipe out." With that said, my worries were laid to rest.

The next morning, I received a phone call at 5:00 am from my husband's doctor. He said, "Mrs. Morrow, where have you been last night? My secretary tried to call you all evening until 12:00 o'clock." (We didn't have voice mail at that time or cellular phones). And I wondered why he called so early, "Mrs. Morrow, if you want to you see your husband, you can come right away, we can't do anything for him and he seems to be slipping away," which meant in coded language – he is dying. Why didn't he say, "Your husband is dying"? Am I afraid of that reality as a minister's wife? I didn't tell the doctor, but I realized that the foreboding presence in my apartment that I ran away from the night before must have been a premonition of death. Is that what mothers or loved ones feel when someone dear to them is in grave danger?

As I put the receiver down, a clergy friend of Denis came to my mind. Should I phone him this early? When I called the Reverend Weeks of Darien, he mentioned that he had just returned from a vacation in England, but told me to

"Wait at the door, or at the bedside, I will be at the hospital in an hour." It took him that long to travel and he telephoned another clergy friend to join him.

We went to see Denis in the ward, but he was still in a coma and his face was red and quite swollen. The two ministers holding hands over the bed were praying and quoting scripture. One of them even took on the role of the patient, "Lord, I Denis ask you to forgive me for…" Is that what ministers do at a deathbed? Suddenly, with eyes still closed he leaned forward on his pillow and dropped back exhausted. I thought "Oh no, this is too much for him. We should leave him alone." I felt uncomfortable and wanted to slip away, but they would not let me. So I was a witness to his healing prayer and Rev. Weeks said, "OK, it is up to the Lord, either He will take Denis home or heal him." Then they grabbed my arms and took me downstairs for a cup of coffee. When we returned the minister asked, "How is OUR patient, Nurse?" "He is fine" and she carried on with her work, but the minister wanted to know more. " Has his fever dropped, how much? " When we entered the room, we found a different person, his face was relaxed, the man in a coma responded with a hand squeeze. That to me was an awesome experience.

And just briefly, Denis was transferred to Gaylord Rehabilitation Hospital in Wallingford, where they did amazing things for his paralysis. He could walk and do chores, like buttoning his shirt. Then they moved him into a nursing home in Branford under Title 19, which I did not realize was a welfare program, under which he received only inferior treatment at BHHCC. I could not afford a private nurse around the clock at home. So I made it a point of visiting him every day after work and spend the evening. It was a special time of blessing for us, perhaps a mini-retirement, because we had every evening to visit and talk. I know, this healing was especially for me.

42. Dixieland - Spring Hill Courier

In the summer of 1976, the Bicentennial year of the United States of America, we moved back to Connecticut into an old parish in Northford. I recall one experience that was obviously another *God-of-the-Splitsecond* event.

It was in the fall of 1981, when my office sent me via shuttle airplane to Washington, DC, to hand-deliver an important document to a federal agency and meet a deadline. Since it was Friday and I was so close to our first parish in Quantico, Maryland, I suddenly felt the urge to hop on a bus and visit our folks, especially since I spent every day in the nursing home with my sick husband in the last year.

Just as I stepped out of the building, having made my urgent delivery on time, I saw a bus standing in front of the entrance. I asked the driver if he could tell me where I could get the Annapolis Bus, mentioning that I wanted to go to Salisbury, Maryland. "Lady, you are on it!" said the bus driver, "and I am leaving in a few minutes." Coincidence, you stubborn skeptics, eh? Miracles do happen even in 1981 and to people like the anxious Thomas that I was myself.

I sat in this "surprise bus" taking me to our old parish on the Eastern Shoreline over the high Chesapeake Bridge at Annapolis. When the bus approached our village of Hebron, I noticed a lot of cars parked in front of the 200-year old church. "Something must be going on," I thought and I asked the bus driver to let me off here. I had no idea that I would arrive just in time for their annual Thanksgiving dinner? But my God knew and set the stage for this refreshing time of fellowship with people I hadn't seen for four years. That was Friday night.

I stayed with one of my dear friends on that weekend and had a wonderful time visiting with several other families. I was going to take a bus back to New York City on Sunday in time to be back at the office Monday morning. My hostess gave me a book to read on the long bus ride to New

Haven and said, "I enjoyed Catherine Marshall's latest book *'Meeting God at Every Turn'* so much, you might like to read it on the way home." And I certainly did, in fact, the bus was almost empty on that Sunday afternoon and I curled up on a double seat and read the whole book during those five hours. I read and cried, and prayed and read some more. I have never seen such a similarity in any writer's experiences before - Catharine's matched mine, how come? God knew that my caretaker soul needed some therapy now - this time from the Great Physician Himself.

Catharine Marshall was the wife of the famous Chaplain Peter Marshall in Congress during World War II and his unique and succinct prayers influenced the Senators and Representatives who were dropping in for a brief prayer session at noon. You may have seen the film "A Man Called Peter".

When I returned from my trip to Maryland, I shared with my husband the great time that I had at our old parish and brought him the many greetings and news. It seemed like he had been there himself. But then he wanted to know what Catharine's book was like and with a slip of the tongue I mentioned how her husband suddenly became ill - I stopped, but he insisted to know the whole story. Peter suddenly became ill one evening and had to be taken to the hospital by ambulance. Catherine with the new baby in her arms could not go with him. "See you in the morning, Catharine!" were Peter's cheerful words. Next morning she arrived with the baby, but Peter had just passed on to glory before she saw him again.

Strange, for about a week or more Denis would say to me, "See you in the morning, Catharine!" instead of his usual goodbye. And in the evening, he would want to know more about our past. In retrospect, he was recalling the blessings and hardships we experienced together. Perhaps it was his way of saying goodbye to me, because one morning I got an early phone call, that he had just passed on to his eternal home.

43. Hold That Scaffold - Another Saint Is Coming

While my husband was at the nursing home, I made arrangements to pick him up every Sunday morning and take him to Christ Church in Guilford. It was a chore to seat a paralyzed person from a wheelchair into the front seat of my Toyota. No special privileges of having a van pick him up instead. He loved being at church and meeting many people and chatting with them at coffee hour.

Denis lived for another year-and-a-half since that miraculous recovery at St. Raphael's. It was a special time of blessing for us, perhaps a mini-retirement for both of us, because we had every evening to visit and talk. I know, this healing was especially for me.

Eventually, his health was fading and he passed away in January 1982. The funeral service was held at Christ Church, a town dating back to 1639, where we worshipped every Sunday. His clergy friend, the Revered Bradford Locke, officiated, but I did not expect such a big representation of clergy there, eight ministers and the Archdeacon from Bridgeport. I was overwhelmed, with my sister from Toronto as the only relative at my side. The rest of my family in Germany could not afford to come.

As I stood there at the graveside as a widow after 15 years almost to the day, I remembered that our walk and life together as "Sojourners" began on an icy cold January day in Toronto in 1967. And now in January, I am saying farewell to continue the journey by myself.

Another unusual thing happened. The tall sanctuary was filled with huge scaffolds reaching to the ceiling. This day, on Monday, the painters were supposed to start painting the tall interior of the sanctuary. But they had to postpone their work and even take the scaffold down, because a saint of

God needed to be escorted to his final resting place. Isn't it like that in life sometimes, that God has to put some action on hold because the church is still under construction, before we can proceed?

44. Gaylord Addendum

This event happened on or about March 21, 1984, and I want to add it to the St. Raphael's story. That was the day, when I won $22,000 in the lottery – not really, but I did FIND that money and it was crucial because it literally saved my house. Why? Two years after my husband died, I received a friendly Christmas letter from the State of Connecticut, saying: "Mrs. Morrow, either you pay us $42,747 in two months or we will foreclose the house!" What was I to do?

This brash notice of eviction dampened my Christmas mood, I didn't feel like putting any decorations up. Instead, I designed a more somber décor for my front lawn. Perhaps this is my last Christmas here, I thought. It was a wooden manger, a cross illuminated with red lights, and a crown with colorful light bulbs.

But I had to act fast, there was no way I could get a loan of $43,000 anywhere, so I hunted for a lawyer to defend my case and the small equity, which was really my family's money and not my husband's portion, which the State wanted to get its hands on. My attorney fought bravely to set the records straight of this widow's wealth, but the State would not budge nor waiver its claim. We reached rock bottom in our legal battle and my lawyer's advice for me was *to stay put and not to sell the house*. Most of all, I didn't want to break my father's heart, who had lost all his possessions twice through the Nazis in World War II, now to see his daughter's legacy grabbed by a greedy welfare government of the United States. So I kept this predicament as a secret from my parents.

What I could not understand, how one year's nursing home care and three months at Gaylord Hospital should cost that much, especially since he was on Title 19. I remember going through the pile of paperwork one night, looking at every item on the IBM printout from Gaylord. "Wow, here is an item of $15,000. What is that for?" I said out loud. I could barely decipher the faint print, but I managed to identify "Blue Cross".

Ok, if Gaylord charged Blue Cross $15,000 and the hospital paid them, why does the government still bill me for it? Or better yet, why is Welfare after me for that money? Could I be onto something? Did Blue Cross pay the hospital and did they collect from Welfare as well? This was a sensitive issue that I needed to check out in person.

At 8:00 am next morning I arrived at Gaylord Hospital in Wallingford, asking to see the accounting supervisor because I needed some records. I was brushed off, saying the files were in archives and they could mail it to me. But I insisted that I must have the records that morning and I would wait in the cafeteria.

When the copies were ready in about an hour, I sat in the accountant's office, glancing over the statement and I noticed – there it is again: $15,000. The supervisor wanted to take another look. "Well, I am not sure," was her reply, so I helped along. "Oh, I can barely read it, could it mean Blue Cross?" to which she reluctantly agreed. I also got out of her that Blue Cross had paid Gaylord for this amount.

That was my moment of defense. "What I can't understand, is how the State of Connecticut wants $43,000 from me, part of it is for Gaylord. And now I learn that Blue Cross paid you. Don't they audit your books periodically? I would think one should notice if there were $15,000 extra in the TILL?"

If I hadn't gone to see Gaylord Hospital that morning, I would still have a debt of $43,000 over my head, while

Gaylord overlooked a double payment. My attorney brought this to the attention of the collection department – but that fraud case must have gotten lost in the political quagmire. No response from Hartford. Nevertheless, I did find the $22,000 (including interest) which I supposedly owed the State. That was my birthday gift on March 22, to have suddenly noticed that accounting "error" the night before.

The Gaylord discovery reminds me of a weekend a few years later, when I heard a terrible explosion in the basement. The furnace had burned a hole in the casing and the furnace wall was red hot with flames leaping out. In addition, that furnace stood very close to the wall and could have started a fire in the house, had I been at my office. So it happening on Saturday was a gracious protection, for which I was thankful. Being winter, the repairman needed to replace the furnace immediately. But he said he couldn't do it unless I'd pay $3,000 in cash. I didn't have that much money in my account. Could I get an equity loan in a day?

The day before I received a printed matter letter from my bank about some matter. I hadn't read it yet and didn't realize what the letter was about until I spoke to my bank representative about the needed loan, when I happened to show her the letter. So that morning I reclaimed $3,000 which I needed that very day, from an inactive account which I had forgotten about. To me that $3,000 find was another *God-of-the-Splitsecond* event in an hour of need.

45. Don't Touch That Televison!

This happened while my husband was in the hospital. My sleep was interrupted by lightning and thunder pounding in quick intervals. I tried to ignore it, so I pulled a pillow over my head, hoping the storm would move away soon. You may know the old method: if you can count one second between the lightning and the thunder, it's about a mile away. Trudy, get up, be ready for an emergency at least for the tenants upstairs. Perhaps I should unplug the radio and the TV?

As I bumbled from my bedroom towards the television to pull out the plug, I was suddenly aware of a warning, almost audibly, "Don't tough that television!" When I moved away from it, startled and surprised, I heard a loud crash in the house and saw a bright flash above the television. "Wow, the cord must have burned!" I thought.

The next day I had an electrician repair the damage. He worked on the switchbox in the basement. Sure enough, there was a black streak down the wiring to the pump, etc. His diagnosis: "Lady, your house got hit by a lightning, the television is only one thing, you need the plumber to do the repairs as well." Amazing, I could have been hit by lightning the moment the current hit the house, but instead the Lord gave me a warning to stay away from the trouble spot. I guess, I was not supposed to pass on just then!

46. Call Me And I Shall Answer

This time I was not even calling on the Lord and I didn't expect an answer, but He did answer in an unexpected way. It was in 1983 or 1984 when I had a terrible bout with the Hong Kong flu. The doctor told me to stay in bed, drink plenty of liquids and put up with it.

But being all alone in the house for a week, I became increasingly weaker. I hadn't eaten for days and could barely get up. Looking across the street I could see my young neighbor as she got into the car. What is her name or her phone number, maybe she could get me some help? I don't know why I did not think of calling the police, or maybe I did try. The 911 number did not exist then, and I was too weak to remember any number to call.

I fell back into bed exhausted and somewhat in a daze. But I still remember my desperate words, "Alright Lord, if I am going to die in this bed, because no one is here to help me, IT WILL BE YOUR FAULT!" How could a person that has experienced so much grace in her life, say something like this? But I did and collapsed into unconsciousness, it seemed. It was Sunday morning, and I dozed in that stupor, just moistening my lips with a sip of water now and then.

Someone must have been knocking at my front door for some time, but I didn't hear it. After persistent loud knocks on my living room window, I heard someone calling, "Trudy, are you in there?" I dragged myself out of bed and looked. Why, this is Ray, my friend from years back, with whom I had been teaching a teen class. What was he doing here – TODAY? I was so surprised.

You guessed it, if you caught on to the method of *God-of-the-Splitsecond* by now. My friend told me that he had been thinking about me a lot and decided to drop by on his way home from church. He saw that I was in serious trouble and ordered an ambulance to the hospital. It turned out that I had walking pneumonia. A good Samaritan helped me out and I was grateful.

47. Right Street, Right House

It was a cold Saturday morning in February of 1984, when I drove into a different neighborhood on my way home from shopping. As I was reading the street names to find my way back, the sign "Briarwood" caught my attention. It suddenly occurred to me, "Isn't that the street where one of the lady lives who visited my husband regularly to read to him in the nursing home?"

You see, as a result of his illness he became virtually blind and there were three women visiting him as readers during the day. I never met them and only learned about them after his death. Well, I lost the address, which one of the women gave me and I couldn't remember her last name.

Why don't I stop at one of the houses on this road and ask for "Alice". But I hesitated because there may be several women with that name living here. Would I look like a fool or get the door slammed for my stupid inquiry?

Maybe I should just try this first house. As I knocked on the door, ready with "I am looking for a friend of mine," I didn't even get to finish this apologetic speech. A lady answered the door and beamed brightly, "Well, Trudy, how nice to see you. What brings you here?" That was something I did not expect, to find the RIGHT person on my first call. She invited me to a cup of coffee, we chatted and I learned more about those reading sessions. What a blessing that awkward visit was for me. Did *God-of-the-Splitsecond* have anything to do with this?

48. Tears for Bosnia

One day at the office in 1991, I dashed out into the hall to deliver some urgent paper to a colleague a few doors down, when I almost bumped into a lady. Our offices were part of a busy thoroughfare between two buildings. You had to dodge your way around a busy stream of people going to and from. I said "excuse me" but I noticed that she had been crying, so I pretended I did not see her tears and went on. But she called me back, "Oh, you work in this office? I believe we have met in the cafeteria," and I sensed that she wanted to talk to me rather than running away from an awkward situation.

What I was about to hear or listen to – was not what you would expect, a confession of some big secret. Instead, she just said to me, "Oh, you will understand!" Now I became curious as she added, "Well, you are a European too, and you can understand better than these Americans." I didn't follow, until she added, "You see, they started to bomb BOSNIA, and my parents and relatives live in Belgrade. I am so worried about them!"

49. Fleurop Express

On a cold day in February, I decided to send a flower arrangement via Fleurop to a friend of mine who had moved to the Midwest, as a "hello" and birthday greeting. We had lost touch with each other for awhile. After a few days I got impatient und picked up the phone to chat with her. Apparently, she and her husband had just sat down for dinner. "No, the flowers have not arrived yet," but as we were talking over the phone, my friend exclaimed, "Wait a minute, there is someone at the door!" Apparently the delivery man didn't want to risk leaving the flowers outside my friend's home to get frost-bitten. So he left them with the neighbor.

"How interesting," my friend said to her neighbor in the doorway, as she opened the gift envelope, "Your name is Morrow as well, and the flowers come from a Mrs. Morrow from Connecticut. In fact, she is on the phone right now. What a strange coincidence!" If the name would have been Smith or Miller I could understand, but a rare name like "Morrow?"

I must say, there were some unexpected aspects to this flower event.

50. Quinnipiac Crash

On my way to work along Interstate 95 one rainy August morning in 1984, I was approaching the Quinnipiac Bridge from which you can overlook the Bay and the City of New Haven. I was driving in one of three lanes, listening to the news on my radio. Suddenly, my thoughts were interrupted by an idea that startled me, almost audibly, "the driver behind you is going to drive into your car!"

I glanced through the rear view mirror and saw an open truck changing into my lane and the passenger yanking the arm of the driver. Perhaps they were in an argument, maybe he was saying "watch out!" What am I to do in this calamity? Again, a quick idea came to me, "put your arm over your eyes and your head on the wheel!" Immediately I obeyed and leaned over the wheel. Next thing I know, my car was hit hard from behind. There was no way to get out of this lane in the busy rush hour traffic on the bridge!

I believe, the Lord conveyed this message to me in the crucial moment. The truck had completely bald tires and just sailed into my station wagon on the wet road, completely bashing in the rear end of my station wagon. The police yelled at that driver, "How can you drive with bald tires like that?" And he said to me, "You are lucky, you would have been killed if you had a small car!" And my whiplash was minor because my head had been resting on the wheel.

That experience really spoke to me and the Lord got my attention, especially by this sudden order just prior to the accident. My *God-of-the-Splitsecond* was graciously protecting me. Rather than wondering why this accident happened, I asked for what purpose it did.

51. That Night He Couldn't Sleep

I am reminded of Queen Esther and the Dinner invitation she gave to King Ahasuerus, her husband, and to Prime Minister Haman. Esther was a perfect hostess and lady, the meal was superb, the company enjoyable. When it came to the desert and the last sip of wine, the King asked, what was on her mind. And I wonder, why she didn't come out with her reason for the dinner, she could have done it ever so tactfully when the King asked. I believe, she planned to express her concern, but something (or someone?) must have restrained her. Because you see, the King needed to do some reading before he would have understood the petition, which Queen Esther wanted to make on behalf of her people. Hadn't she asked her uncle Mordecai beforehand for prayer support and fasting of her people, the Israelites? It was no small matter, for the fate of her Hebrew people and her own life was at stake. Did she turn coward at the dinner table?

Esther had to make the awkward proposition of inviting these two people again to dinner the next day, hoping she would say it then. Didn't she realize that the King had a busy schedule and may not be able to come back so soon?

Anyway, my attention is drawn to the sleepless night the King had and the unusual request he made to his servant to read him the records, the Minute-Book of Events, if you please. Couldn't he have asked for some novel or for a soothing harp solo, or whatever? I can see God's hand in this, bringing up the astonishing report of Mordecai who had saved the King's life at one time. And that bit of information changed history and the course of the second dinner. Which reminds me of a sleepless night I had that was somewhat unusual.

52. Baby Dolls in the Canal

In the summer of 1983 I had a rather unusual dream, a real nightmare, because I woke up from it horrified and wondering what it would mean.

In that dream I saw myself walking along a canal, much like the one near my parents' home in Hannover, Germany, and I was walking with my youngest sister, who was holding her young child by the hand. But she talked to me so excitedly that she somehow ignored the child and it must have slipped away. All of a sudden she said, "Where is my child?" We thought it was playing and picking flowers at the slope of the canal. In horror, I said, "Maybe it fell into the canal. Let's look for it."

Both of us were frantically scanning the water and dipped our hands into the stream, but we only came up with dolls, dolls, and more dolls. Then we noticed that there was a floodgate with a walk above it. If the child had drowned, it would be stopped there. Again, as I leaned over and reached into the water, I only pulled up dolls, no child in sight.

I woke up with the horrible thought, that I must have distracted a mother from her duties, and now this child is drowned – dead. How awful! Why did I dream this, maybe one of my nieces or nephews is in danger? So I prayed, "Lord, please help this child, whoever it is. Please save it from dying!" And I was ready to turn over and go back to sleep, realizing that the Almighty God is in charge of this crisis.

But I was not going to get away that easy. I felt very guilty that I was so superficial in passing this tragedy so quickly in prayer. It seemed like God was saying, "I want you to labor in prayer and really intercede. There IS a child in danger." So I followed the inner prompting, sat up in bed and prayed intensely, I lost track of time. But then I needed to get some sleep to be able to function in the office in the morning.

Shortly after I arrived at the office, I got a call from Personnel, saying that a staff member had recently arrived from Germany with his family and needed a stenographer for some urgent typing. Would I come right away with pen and pad? So I dropped my translation work and went to the new staff member's office.

After a brief introduction and small talk, this young man rapidly dictated his text while paving the floor restlessly. Occasionally, he stopped to look out of the window for some concentration, I thought. Then he mentioned almost like talking to himself that he found it hard to get his thoughts together because his little girl was in the hospital and her life is in danger. Wow! Was that why I was in such agony last night? Of course, it would have been out of place to disclose to him my "fitting dream experience". I merely expressed my sympathy and continued taking his dictation.

But my typing was spiced with amazement and a prayer that God would help this family and the little girl in the hospital. For me that incident was another *God-of-the-Splitsecond* sign that He, the Great Physician, works day and night.

Part III

New England Vision

I call this experience my "Civic Awakening". My knowledge of American history and our Christian heritage
was primitive and superficial. Peter Marshall's books
among others created an interest of inquiry into the real
American dream and legacy, thus opening up a new venue
of discovery.

   In this section alone are 16 stories of "God-of-the-
Splitsecond" events, showing me in different ways that the
Lord cares, that He knows where I am, what I need, what
He wants me to do in my life. It is these stories, that my
nieces and nephews asked me to write down in a family
book so they would have them for their children, I only
have "children of my heart."

   These events are intertwined with my calling to do
"Apologetics for Teens" and to write educational material. They are illuminated with the epoch-making event
of the Berlin Wall coming down in 1989 and the collapse
of Communism. Since then we have progressed to "9-ll"
of the Twin Towers, and a whole new perspective on the
world.

53. Hartford Capitol and the Con-Con

One day I found a little postcard from an unknown person in my mailbox, an invitation to attend a hearing at the Capitol in Hartford on March 18, 1985. Thinking this must be a mistake, I phoned this person. A lady answered and told me more about that event concerning the Constitutional Convention, also known as Con-Con. I had never been to any hearing, so I went along with the group. I was impressed with the magnificent architecture of the Capitol building and learned that it is a rare landmark.

The grand hallway is like a beautiful museum with tokens of Connecticut's unique history. There is even a copy of the Liberty Bell in the hall. I milled around as a tourist after signing my name at the front door with the other people. The large Senate Room was filling up to capacity and people were standing in the hallway. I was an ignorant observer whose attention had been aroused. Since I also write shorthand, I kept taking notes of the things that were so educational.

Having spent one weekend recently with a challenging book, entitled "The Second American Revolution" by John Whitehead, and pouring over another book by Peter Marshall "The Light and the Glory," my mind was alert and interested in what was going on, but I had no idea that because I signed my name on that list in the Senate Hall, I may be called upon to speak – horrors, I would get stage fright.

I spent the entire day just milling around the Capitol, admiring the beautiful sculptures and frescos, while the

Con-Con hearing was going on all day. The crowd of citizens thinned out by the evening, I sat in the back of the Senate room listening. All of a sudden, someone announced "we have time for one more person before we close – the next name is Trudy Morrow." "Oh my God," I thought, "what now?" Hesitantly I walked to the front, after I had been admiring the large oil painting on the wall looming over the Senate seats, depicting Madison and the Founding Fathers signing in Philadelphia. I don't remember the exact words, but I said something like:

"We have been listening to many petitions today. I do not want to repeat what has been said, but I want to express what I feel this day at this historic place. It speaks to me in the painting above our heads, in the actions of these brave foresightful men, to create a land, a nation of freedom and for freedom.

And I as one who has come a long way from the harrowing roads of oppression and fear of Nazism and the War, am privileged to be standing here tonight. May our actions be those of vigilant citizens of One Nation Under God. And with this thought, I bid you Good Night!"

I walked down silently, amazed that I should be there speaking as the last person of the day.

54. Mac, the Gutenberg Press

Eventually the need became apparent to me to own an electric typewriter so that I could do some writing and especially translations which was my profession at that time. The salesman looked at me surprised to learn that I wanted another IBM. "Well, we use word processors at the office (the grandfather of PC), but I can't afford one yet." But the salesman led me to a display of a tiny grey box which he picked up by the handle. What is this?" I asked surprised. And the salesrep replied, "That's an Apple computer, the new K-512, and here is the printer for it." I waved my hand, "No I can't afford that."

But I was so impressed with the little box that day and I plunged into the world of personal user-friendly Macs. It changed my life. If my philosopher, thinking-type father would have lived to see the day, it would have been a wonderful blessing for him. We have volumes of his handwritten letters and meticulous papers on the books he read, on thoughts he pondered about. He died before desktop-publishing arrived, when you can "cut and paste", edit, enlarge and move text easily. But I am reminded of the thought somebody expressed:

"If Moses had a computer instead of tables of stone, the Ten Commandments would not have been better, only lighter."

This is an admonition to my own heart to use this tool wisely, and that an expensive equipment does not warrant wisdom.

55. The Writer's Tree

There is an attractive tree carved out of olive wood on my dresser, which is a gift of a friend of mine for whom I was privileged to type her books on my first computer – the little Macintosh K-512. You see, my friend Virginia was a real writer who kept journals and shoeboxes of notes on things which she one day intended to put into that legacy book for her grandchildren, as she said. I got to know and appreciate her, what a beautiful person! She wanted to hear more of my stories, some of those you are reading here – but I was really a Literary Jonah. Somebody said, that if all the thinkers would write, and the writers would think, we'd have better books and less of them. I just didn't get to my book YET.

One day I received a call at my desk at Yale Medical from my friend, and she asked me to come over to her ward. As she greeted me, I asked jokingly, "What are you doing here, Virginia? And what is this box on your lap?" She sat up holding a shoebox filled with notes and a yellow pad and said: "Trudy, remember the LEGACY BOOK that I was going to write for my grandchildren? Here it is. Can you please type as fast as you can and bring me the draft tomorrow?"

She must have sensed that her time was short, although the doctors were still looking for the cause of her malaise. The thought ran through my head, "Trudy, if you had to go to the hospital today, where would your work be?" (In my head so far).

From that moment on in July, I wrote feverishly until November. I'd pick up notes from her bedside, go home, type in the evening – even get up after some short sleep – and type, in order to have the drafts or the corrections ready for her the next day. And I would go to pick up more work because she was still writing about a chapter ahead of me. Eventually the doctors found the cause: cancer, and they told her that she had only a very short time to live.

My friend asked to be allowed to stay in her home with a nurse. It was unusual for me to visit a dying friend. I know she did not put up a front because she lived day by day in the strength of her Lord and Savior. She still had so much to give and she had such peace.

But her strength was waning quickly, so her girlfriend took over the role of editor and both of us worked on the text. When the manuscript was finally ready for printing with all the pictures in place, she brought it to the patient in the hospice. Virginia hugged her legacy book and said "Oh, Lord, the book is finished!" And two days later she passed on.

I had no idea that I was to inherit this carved olive tree from her with removable leaves and apples. But her son brought it to me and I know what that gift meant to me. It's the Appleseed's Tree for the Literary Jonah. (My vision at that time was to write stories for children as "Appleseed's Wit")

56. Literary Jonah

The longer I live, the more I realize, much to my dismay, that the title applies to me. It is another fifteen years since the "Writer's Tree" and I am still wrestling with that stubborn Jonah-nature. And my agony is not spent on the very book "God-of-the-Splitsecond", which is really a response to my niece Anita's request, "Tante Trudy, please write these things you experienced down for us, so that we can read them to our children." Her generation did not live through the turmoil of World War II, the deportation from our homeland, the refugee time etc. She is a child of the post-TV, postmodern, post-a-lot-of-things generation. But I understood what she meant that as a family member, whom she trusts not to manufacture these marvelous stories, I should write them down for a family history.

The agony of the Literary Jonah had a different cause, the conviction on her heart that she should and could produce educational material for children and youth in a shorter, simpler form to portray the essence of an idea, like an "Appleseed" being the essence of a tree. Like a translation of some profound wisdom, but with short practical "Wit" for the young.

So Lady-Jonah would browse through bookstores and libraries for this type of literature or material over months and years. She has not found it yet. She even prayed, "Lord, if this idea is my own ambition and dream, then please take this burden way from me. I want to go on with life." I have reviewed many books, worked my way through many exhibits, and what-not, but I have not found anyone replacing my vision – so that I could get it out of my mind.

Meanwhile, other things equally as challenging have come about in the nature of teaching kids and in the meantime there are many productions on the Internet. Instead "this Old House", my Old Victorian, continues to make its distracting demands of upkeep, such as the arduous work in "the Chaco" and the overgrown wilderness overtaking my lawn (see my story on the "Berlin Express" of 1000 Mennonites escaping from the Soviets to settle in Paraguay).

Thus I find the answer to my Jonah-odyssey in handling what is right before me, one literary thing at a time as I am dealing with life in its many challenges and opportunities. We call this Divine PROVIDENCE. I'd like to remember one of the lessons I learned from my Anglican husband. As Christians we are given the privilege to walk between two pillars:

MERCY and GRACE.
Mercy is God NOT giving us what we deserve.
GRACE is God giving us what we DON'T deserve.

57. Octagonal Vision

It started with a window project in 1993 at my Old Victorian house, that real estate which keeps me busy as a "Carpenter Maid" for the last 30 years. This time I delegated the work to some professionals and I had two men lined up for a Saturday afternoon. I needed to have one of the tall 5 ft Georgian windows replaced with a small octagonal one in order to gain some wall space. I wanted to make sure it was being done right. Well, none of them showed up, they must have found some bigger jobs. Will I have to do it after all?

I remember that awful feeling in my stomach, that "This Old House" was a terrible slave driver. Why did I put up with it for so long? It robs me of my energy, time and money.

OK, this is the last time I will do any major work on it, I decided. But how do you put an octagonal window in for now? I remember agonizing over it and crying all along. I have never cried over any job before. With every nail I drove into the wall, I seemed to express, that this window will be a reminder that I am finished with the demands of this house. No longer will I bow under this heavy load. From now on I will work on the "Department of the Interior" and devote more time to reading and people and caring for the inner person.

When I reclined to go to bed, tired and worn out, I remember the shape of the window occupying my mind: "octagonal", "octave", "octavian", and I became curious about the meaning of these words. So I slipped into my the library to check in the dictionary.

"Octave" is an ecclesiastical term, meaning the age of the church, or the eighth day of creation. It also means perfect harmony in musical terms. And the thought implied to me that there must be harmony in our lives and in our society. We are wrong in separating church and state – in fact, it is impossible and schizophrenic. The sacred and the secular, the spiritual and the physical are part of one inseparable reality.

Without going into further detail, it was at that weekend that my writing ministry crystalised into objective form and goals, and I was led to consider establishing an educational institute, whose name was derived from these words. But "Octave Institute" was awkward, so I chose "Octavia Institute". So there you have it, at least the birthpangs of an educational ministry, which I believe, the Lord has laid on my heart. And I will spare you the *God-of-the-Splitsecond* factor, which I decided to keep to myself. Lateron I changed the name to "Otawit Institute" because the word "Octavia" was used frequently in connection with occult and secular endeavors.

58. Olivia Slept Here

Shortly after the Octagonal Window experience, I made plans to get stationary and business cards for the newly created Octavia Institute. A friend of mine asked me to give her a ride to the airport near Hartford, which is about an hour away.

On my way back I wanted to sightsee the city and I drove up to the Capitol, an impressive unique building surrounded with statues of famous New Englanders, i.e. John Davenport, Timothy Dwight, Governor Bradford, John Trumbull, John Winthrop and others. I noticed a big crowd assembled in the park nearby, so I stopped to see what was going on and listen to the speaker. A lady tapped me on my shoulder and said something. I don't know how we got into a conversation, but I mentioned that it was an important week for me. "I just started a desktop company" and handed her my brand-new business card. She replied "Octavia Institute? That sounds almost like my name, it's Olivia. I'll pray for your company that the Lord will bless it." I smiled and walked away. She doesn't know me, but I appreciate her effort.

As I drove home, I remembered that I must show up at the youth program in the evening where a visiting high school team from Moody presented a play at our church. I volunteered to have two girls from the group as my guests overnight. The play was very interesting and I noticed that the leading actress was "Olivia". Strange, I met somebody with that name today. Wouldn't it be strange, if Olivia were designated to be my house guest tonight?

After the play, I waited in the hall with other hostesses to take our charges. Guess what, one of the two ladies assigned to me was indeed Olivia. Of course, I did not tell her about my preceeding thoughts. Next morning, we spent a leisurely time on the porch and got to know each other before that group went on to the next place with their performance.

59. Good Samaritan, New York Style

This event borders on the miraculous, it was certainly an unusual experience for me. It started out as an enjoyable ride in my Toyota-Corola along the Merritt Parkway with my sister and brother-in-law from Germany, whom I was taking back to the J.F. Kennedy Airport. We had a wonderful time together as we drove in my tough little Toyota some 2000 miles along the east coast all the way to Savannah, Georgia. Upon my return, my mechanic checked the car thoroughly and said it was in good shape.

We had a lovely ride on the Merritt Parkway and we enjoyed the brilliant autumn foliage of our maples, something Europeans admire especially. I waved a last good-bye to them as they walked through the gate to their airplane and I headed to my car to get back to New England. As soon as I got out of the parking lot, I found myself in heavy traffic which got worse on the 8-lane highway as we inched along about 2 miles an hour, I was listening to my radio. As I approached the first underpass, my car suddenly stopped and the lights went out. I was in the far left lane. I was hoping that a police cruiser would notice my dilemma and come to my aid. I waved and relied on my AAA sign, nobody bothered.

I must have been stalled there for an hour, when I began to feel sick to my stomach from the fumes of the traffic. My car was trapped beneath an overpass and I felt increasingly nauseated. Suddenly panic gripped me: "Trudy, nobody is going to stop here, unless you get out of the car and walk. You are going to die here of carbon monoxide poisoning." At that time another police car passed by and ignored my waiving and hollering. That was it. I broke down in tears and cried, "Lord Jesus, you know that I am sitting here and that I am feeling sick. Whatever is Your will, I have no one to help me but YOU. "

About five minutes later, a car next to me honked and an old man asked: "Are you stuck, do you want us to help you?" And old man behind the wheel, an old lady sitting next to him and an old man leaning out the back window. They looked trustworthy, though. "Yes, thank you, I need help." Thus started the most amazing rescue mission I have experienced by three people who might as well have been angels. They were Romanian-Americans who had just dropped a relative from Europe off at the airport like I did. The man was a taxi driver during the week and knew this dangerous neighborhood of Jamaica (suburb of New York).

His plan was to push my car across four lanes and then uphill the ramp to a gasoline station 50 feet away. His brother got out of the car and stood in front of the traffic lane by lane, so that we could move diagonally to the outer lane. This old man was putting his body in danger – for me? Then they took me into their car and drove around the blocks to look for a telephone booth. His wife noticed one, but the driver said, "You wouldn't get out here if your life depended on it." We finally saw a telephone booth that seemed safe to him. He stood next to me while I called AAA to send for a truck. "Ask for the name of the pickup truck!" he told me, because I might be approached by a "pirate truck" to rob me or worse?! And before my "guardian angels" left, they instructed me to sit in the locked car and look busy, write or do something.

The truck came and pulled my car to his garage, but the other mechanic had already left the shop, so I was supposed to stay overnight. "Lord, I am in a jungle here, please protect me." I stepped outside the garage to wait for a taxi and noticed a sign across the street: "Strauss Stores". Now why in the world do I see my maiden name here? Well, how about as a sign that He sees His frightened "sheep" in New York city?

The taxi brought me to a hotel and the lobby looked alright, but I noticed two couples standing around and the clerk asked me, "You need a room, for how many hours?

The next one is available at 11:00 pm." I didn't register the philosophy behind this, but as I glanced at the price list, I thought, "Wait a minute, Trudy, you are in the wrong place. This must be a brothel." With a subtle smile I answered the clerk, "No thank you, I can't wait, can you please order me a taxi?" And I stepped into the darkened street.

A police car approached and I flagged it down. "Please, help me, I am a stranded Connecticut woman, my car broke down and is in repair. I need a reputable hotel, the Marriot or Holiday Inn, if need be." The policeman was a woman and she was sympathetic, realizing my dilemma. She waved down another taxi and asked him to take me to a good hotel. But the taxi chose to take the long route and drive me right across town to Laguardia to make a few more bucks, I suppose. Nevertheless, in what was one of my toughest "city jungle" experiences, I am thankful for the divine and human help of *God-of-the-Splitsecond*".

60. Pentecost Revisited

The Billy Graham Crusade came to Connecticut in May of 1986 and was held in the big Civic Center in Hartford. Strangely, the event was not advertised on the neon sign outside, you wonder why? On the last Sunday, which happened to be Pentecost, I invited a good friend of my deceased husband to join me and drive to the Crusade. We were quite moved by the powerful message of the day. On our way home, I invited Ryan for a cup of coffee to my home. We sat and looked through old pictures and were reminiscing about days gone by. In this uplifting moment I felt free to ask him, "Do you want to listen to one of Denises sermon tapes?" He replied, "Oh yeah, put one of them on – let's listen!" You see, I hesitated to listen to any of those tapes before, because I was afraid to hear his voice. Today with some one else sitting next to me, I felt safe to try.

So I went to the drawer and just randomly pulled out one of his sermons and put it on the audio tape-player, then sat down, and we both heard his introductory words: "Today is Pentecost, the birthday of the church. Let me tell you a story. I was flying to Chicago and my neighbor started talking. He said he hoped the Jet Stream was in his favor so that he could get to his appointment in time." And then Denis used this comment to make his point: "You see, the Holy Spirit is like the Jet Stream. If you are going with Him in the same direction, he will amplify your life, but if you are heading in the opposite direction, you will have a hard time."

I didn't want to interrupt this brief illustration while the tape was playing and I listened to my husband's voice for the first time since several years. At the end of this message I told my friend sitting there, that out of dozens of tapes in the drawer, I happened to have randomly picked out this one –coincidentally? We were both amazed at this.

<u>PS. 1995 – nine years later</u>

In October of that year I decided to write a book for my husband's Australian family and I chose the title: "Morrow, Two Sojourners in America". As I attached some copies of photos and memorabilia, I thought it might be a good idea to include some sermon notes. But which one out of several volumes of handwritten binders should I choose? I didn't have time to read them all, so I randomly picked one of the binders and hastily pulled out one with the heading: "GRACE". And I made a copy of this text.

Then I thought it might be good to add one of my husband's sermon tapes to the collection, so that they could hear his voice. I didn't feel like going through a bunch of tapes and reviewing them, I suppose it was tenderness of heart. So I randomly picked a couple of them out of the collection that just showed dates and code numbers. When I played the first tape, I was surprised. Why, out of all things, this tape talks about "Grace"! I thought I should take a closer look at the sermon on paper and listen to the tape as well. Sure enough, it was the same message.

Can you see another "coincidence" or does God have a sense of humor in the way we are sometimes shepherded, not on the hills of Samaria or Judea, but in our own little happenings by our *God-of-the-Splitsecond*.

61. Christmas and the Hill

On a pre-Christmas Saturday in 1987, I had written many Christmas cards and letters to my friends. In order to speed up the mailing, I headed for the main post office in New Haven. On my way downtown, I stopped my car on Temple Street at the Green to see the lights on the tall Christmas tree. They were spectacular. "I am glad I made this detour to admire this festive display", I thought. Somebody walked up the steps into the Davenport Church. "Why not go inside as well to meditate on the real meaning of Christmas and see the decorations inside?" The candles in the window and the altar decoration had such a mystic glow in the darkness. I hadn't expected such peaceful solitude.

My eyes glanced over the many inscriptions in the back of the sanctuary. How many Christmases ago were people worshipping the Christchild and the Savior in this holy place? Wow, this is where the first Puritan settlers landed in 1638 and built their first church under the leadership of John Davenport. I had forgotten so much, but standing on the actual ground of history and reading these plaques, my thoughts turned to Denis and his love for early American history. "Thank you, Lord, for bringing us to this New Haven of ours!"

But I still had a bunch of Christmas letters in my hand that needed to be mailed. That's why I came down to New Haven. No, I won't go to Long Warf anymore, I can drop these letters on the way home at the Branford Post Office, I thought. Coming down Branford Hills on Route 1 just before Wendy's Restaurant, my thoughts were suddenly interrupted with this idea: "Turn right, drive up to Branford Hills Health Care Center!" "Why?" (I had never gone down that street nor entered BHHCC since Denis died five years ago). In this splitsecond order, I also understood that I was supposed to walk inside the building and say "Hi" to the caretakers there. "Why now?" I argued and looked at my old dirty clothes, "Because I want you to meet your pain head-on," was the answer to my soul. "Ok, I'll drive to that nursing home," I responded with a reluctant heart, swung the car sharp to the right and drove uphill. I looked at the watch and it was a few minutes to 8:00 pm (closing time) and I was hoping that I would get there too late, so that I wouldn't have to go inside.

Turning into the parking lot at BHHCC, I noticed from a distance that there were people coming out of that building. A young man was pushing another man in a wheelchair and was heading for a station wagon. He held a Bible in his hand. Strange, a Christian who is demonstrating his faith, I thought. Ignoring these signs, I called out of my car. "Is the nursing home still open?" He answered, "No, they just closed." Trudy, you are off the hook, you don't have to go inside to meet "your pain." But what have we here? Like a lightning flash it dawned upon me, why I was urged to drive uphill, not for the caretakers sake, but to see a man pushed in a wheelchair. Five years and 5 seconds later? Is the *God-of-the-Splitsecond* arranging another event, and for what purpose this time?

While the two young men were getting the handicapped person into the station wagon, I collected my poise to ask the man with the Bible in his hand a question before he would drive away. "I suppose you know the Lord?" And he replied enthusiastically, "Yes, we love Jesus." Pointing to the young man in the wheelchair, I asked, "Are you taking him home for the night?" "Yes, we have a Christmas party for students at our apartment."

When I asked, "Do you come to the nursing home often?" he answered, "We hold a Bible Study here every Saturday. We are believers." So I mellowed, "I used to be here every night, when my husband was a patient. He was a minister." (which I threw in as a bait) "Oh, then you know Jesus too?" This was too much for me. "Why don't you follow our car and come to our Christmas party!" I had forgotten about my shabby clothes I wore as I followed them. What a surprise, I found myself spending a cheerful evening with young "brothers and sisters in Christ", strangers with whom I had much in common.

Now I could see why the sudden prompting to drive "Up the Hill" was from the Lord as a healing measure for my widow-heart. He brought it to the surface that evening that, unless I am willing to meet these nursing home caretakers and forgive them, I am not really free of my pain. And to dramatize that difficult climb, the Lord arranged for a few signs. Had I not been obedient, I would not have run into that wheelchair patient and those Christians. During the entire 15 months when I spent every evening at BHHCC, I never met any group like this and there was no Bible study at the center at that time to my knowledge. Since I avoided that nursing home before, I would not likely have run into this scene until that Christmas evening.

62. Babushka in the Field (story repeated)

The most dramatic *God-of-the-Splitsecond* event, in my opinion, is this one, because of the unusual circumstances surrounding it and the timing, namely 50 years and 5 seconds later, as I call it. I named the title of this book by this event.

It happened in the spring of 1991, when a busload of Germans went on a tour to their homeland in Eastern Europe (Poland and the Ukraine) which had been under Soviet control since 1940 and had been inaccessible since that time. Hitler then forcefully removed hundreds of thousands of ethnic Germans from their homeland and our family was among these. We were put into freight trains like cattle (or chattels?) and relocated by the Nazis into one of the empty Polish homes, from which they previously deported the Poles or Jews and sent them to German labor camps. However, our forced stay in the Warthegau (captured Poland) was only brief, because five years later in 1945 we had to flee from the Russian front heading towards West Germany.

So none of us had seen our original homeland in Galizia since 1940. The memory of the Germans in our homeland had been erased by changing town names and removing records, the Communists (Soviets) also took away anything worthwhile, even frames of houses, machinery, bricks, etc. and shipped it to Russia. Then they combined the whole village into one huge "kolchos". Each farmhouse had only a tiny yard about 30 feet deep left for themselves. The rest of their land was taken from the Soviets and they became laborers in the kolchos.

Here in 1991 is a busload of people trying to visit their towns and villages after 50 years. My cousin Lilly and her husband were among them and they had maps and photos with them. The bus driver who organized this trip was Polish. He was driving along dirt roads trying to find our village named "Theodorshof" or the Polish equivalent name. But they found no signs and the road along fields was muddy and bumpy. In the distance they saw an old woman what they call "Babushka" with her headscarf, carrying a large basket with vegetables and walking along the road. The bus driver stopped and asked her in Polish: "Babushka, where is the town of ......?" A puzzled look – maybe the name of the town had been changed in the meantime, the driver thought.

But my cousin had the presence of mind, she leaned out the doorway and called in German "Where are the graves of Strauss and Mueller?" (which were our mutual grandfathers). The bus driver translated this into Polish, when the old woman beamed and pointed excitedly to an overgrown hill at the end of the field, that cemetery was not visited for 50 years. The driver asked Babushka to step inside the bus, so she could guide them along to the village. "Oh, you are his grandchild? I remember Mr. Strauss and also Mr. Mueller very well, I grew up in the same village." They also learned that she was one of the two families who had NOT been evacuated by the Soviets from that town and replaced by strangers in the Communist shuffle.

Here is the amazing fact: If the bus had taken another route or some another road, they would not have met Babushka. If Babushka had decided to go to the field on another day, or at a different hour, they would not have met her. Was it just a coincidence that SHE was there, and not just any stranger or neighbor from that town? Can you see God in action, fifty years and five seconds later? This event was just as good as if I had been there in person instead of my cousin, and it tells me that the God of History is the God of Providence, the One who loves and cares for me (and for you). Praise be to the *God-of-the-Splitsecond*.

63. Kiev and the Accordion

This event ties in with the Babushka event – like a double action. You see, I did not intend to make this tour to my homeland in Galizia, especially since my cousin Lilly had such a wonderful experience a few years earlier. To me it was as good as if I had been there, but I guess the Lord had something else planned.

In August of 1995, a guest speaker from the Ukraine mentioned that he would be happy to take clothing and medication back to Kiev. Strange that my old accordion came to mind and I wondered if they could use it? I had played it in childrens- and youth ministry in Germany and lateron in my husband's church. Somehow I couldn't make myself sell it or throw it away. The speaker and his wife were delighted about my offer, yes one of their Ukranian students would just love to get the Accordion. "And what are you doing?" asked the speaker, "Oh, I work in the office." "No, I mean what are your interests or what is your ministry?" "Oh, I am interested in education, I read a lot." "Mmh, what authors?" This man was the principal of this new Christian university in Kiev.

I began to feel uncomfortable, and when I tossed out "Francis Schaeffer" and his ideas about "Faith and Reason", he was interested. As I tried to shake hands and walk away, he said, "May I invite you to give a lecture on that subject, that's just what we need in Kiev." I mumbled something like,

"Thank you for the offer, but..." and I created a barrage of excuses. Suddenly it dawned upon me, why this "Balaam-passage." It seemed like the Lord was saying to me, "Trudy, he is not asking you to teach, I AM. You keep reading, and reading, now I have an assignment for you with REAL people, who need to hear this." The principal asked me to send a position paper and a syllabus and the next few months were really challenging for me to prepare for this task, and my church supported some of my financial needs as well.

At Christmastime I composed a humorous letter about my accordion "Gloria-Hohner", which read like adoption papers for the donation of my instrument to Kiev. I also mentioned that Gloria's infancy was spent at TBC in 1956 (now called Tyndale College) and her first teacher was Dixi Dean from the radio station HCJB in Quito, Equador. He also knew the five Auca missionaries from Wycliffe Bible Translators, who were martyred that year. And I added that "Gloria" was now drafted into missionary services after lingering away in a forgotten corner in Trudy's basement.

Well, just two weeks later after this letter was mailed to friends, I attended a large Evangelical conference in Boston called "Congress 96" along with some 6000 people. Elisabeth Elliot, one of the Auca widows, happened to be one of the speakers there, but I was too busy exploring the 300 book displays all day and couldn't attend any of the workshops. At about 3:00 pm I dragged my heavy bags to an eating place just to get something before I would drive home to New Haven.

As I munched on my sandwich, an older man asked me to save the two empty chairs "until I can find my wife". They eventually took their seats at our table and somebody else approached the charming lady by saying "Mrs. Elliot, could we ...?" My ears perked up, I had just finished telling my Christian neighbors at the table that I was going to Kiev and was holding that Gloria-adoption paper in my hand, the paper that just happened to mention the Auca missionaries. I was stunned, here I have been at this huge conference all day and I didn't run into ANY of our 17 people from my home church. Instead, I meet Mrs. Elliot, because her husband happened to select the same table in this big hall – just by coincidence? I had never met this author before. What did *God-of-the-Splitsecond* have in mind this time?

I did fly to Kiev in May of 1996 to teach apologetics to those Ukranian students who were preparing for the ministry on the subject of "Faith and Reason" based on Francis Schaeffer's book. I had to teach one sentence at a time as I was being translated into Russian. It soon became obvious to me why I was supposed to go to Kiev for that brief ministry, not just as an American, but a person whose faith-journey had gone through different crises too, like the underground church in Nazi Germany. But most of all, the illustrations I drew on the large blackboard seemed to be the mode most helpful in the presentation – like mental pictures or windows to grasp an idea. And these graphic illustrations are what I was producing for Octavia Institute (now Otawit Institute).

It was indeed an unforgettable time for me to meet these young Ukranian students, whose education had been carved out and manipulated by Communism for so long. They wanted to catch up with history and learn to think within the framework of God's truth and reality. I discovered that one of the students even had a brief biography of Francis Schaeffer in a Russian translation.

What a privilege it was for me to be asked to lecture to these sincere people and their dedication to learning. Also, this time I was "forcefully" brought to Eastern Europe, not to be confiscated by the Communists in 1945 and shipped to Siberia (see my story "Lost and Found"), but by the loving hand of God to give me some concrete "internship" task as a philosopher-in-training and a believer, who could relate to them somehow because of the hardships we had experienced.

64. Appleseed's Square

This true story relates to the previous "Kiev and the Accordion" account. And especially in regard to meeting the writer Elisabeth Elliot for the first time at the Conference in Boston in January 1996 who happened to sit down at my lunch table with her husband. The lunch could have been a coincidence, if I hadn't written the "Gloria Hohner" story about my accordion earlier and referred to the Auca missionaries just minutes earlier. Granted, a skeptic might find some explanation for that. But what would he make of the following little incident in Boston?

I drove up to Boston in my car and was looking for an exit off the Highway I-295. I was planning to spend a day at the Gordon-Conwell Library, where I wanted to do some research. The directions I received were unclear. I thought I had missed the exit, so I decided to turn off at the next exit and find a telephone. At the ramp I found a mall and the sign read "Appleseed's Square." "Nice, for the writer of Appleseed's Wit," I thought. I got new directions, found the Gordon Library and spent a whole day there. It was dark and raining at 7:00 pm and I had to think about driving home again to Connecticut.

I made my way carefully through the campus to get back to the beltway and I followed the directions someone just gave me. But I got caught in a horrendous downpour of rain and heavy fog. I could not see a sign or read the street names in that wooded area. There was no one to ask. My gas tank was almost empty and I could barely see beyond the dashboard. Will I be stranded here in the cold night? After 20 minutes of bumbling through the wooded countryside in torrents of rain, I ended up at "Appleseed's Square" AGAIN to my great surprise after driving blind! Or was Someone directing my path?

Sure enough, I made it home safely and thanked *God-of-the-Splitsecond* for His gracious protection on that long and difficult ride.

65. Victorian Ghost Stories

There seemed to be a chain of events with an unusual pattern worth mentioning and they happened within a year. I think I know the cause of these "interferences", but I am not at liberty to mention it here. They had to do with water and plumbing and happened only when members of my German family visited with me. So I call them the "German Water Falls".

German Water Falls - Phase I.

When my oldest nephew from Hannover and his girlfriend were visiting with me, I was awakened one morning, as they yelled, "Come quickly, Tante Trudy! Water is running down from the kitchen ceiling!" It was pouring down between the cracks and out of the ceiling lights. There was a leak in the tenant's bathroom above, which I had immediately fixed, thinking the problem was solved.

The two visitors continued on their photo-safari in Vermont and New Hampshire to capture the magnificent autumn sceneries for their professional portfolio. Voila!

German Water Falls - Phase II.

The next year, I had two visitors from Hannover again, this time my youngest nephew and his girlfriend Tatjana, with whom I spent some wonderful time and we milled through the vast and interesting Yale University campus. On the day they were to fly home, I woke up hearing one of them yell, "Tante Trudy, there is water running down the kitchen ceiling. Help!" This time it must have been seeping through for awhile because the ceiling was soaked. The same plumbing problem from the upstairs bath. This time I had pipes replaced and even the kitchen plumbing redone.

German Water Falls - Phase III.

There was yet another incident waiting to surprise me, and this one was more subtle and more expensive than the other two, costing about $2,000.

It also was during the visit of my niece and her German husband and their little baby girl came to spend some time with me. At the end of the visit, they took me out to dinner. When we came back we found that we had NO water. How can that be? My niece's husband happened to be a plumber. He inspected the situation and found that the pump was not working because the well motor had burned out. I remember hearing the toilet tank running as we left in a hurry for the restaurant, but could a little dribbling have caused all that?

Consequently, I called my local plumber who had to climb into the outside well and replace the 72 feet pump - to the tune of $2,000.

66. Appleseed's Dilemma

Apparently the water episode was just the beginning of a rough time ahead for me with my tenants (i.e. the next ones to move in). Thinking that I rented the upstairs apartment to a family of three, I discovered that they sneaked in seven beds and moved a group of five into the premises. They didn't pay their rent and were destructive, so I had to evict them eventually.

That was the last straw for me. I really had enough of "This Old House" and was seriously looking for a cozy small apartment or a little ranch somewhere. I felt I had reached the end of my road after 20 years of renovating and fixing this Old House up without an end in sight. Now, as my energies were dwindling, I had better make a smart move to a place that would not wear me out but free my mind to build a "mental house" so-to-speak, and to continue with my WRITING.

Now I seriously thought about selling, but the realtors didn't help much, so I decided to put a sign out on the front yard "For Sale By Owner". I was amazed at the good response, but somehow it didn't sell at a worthwhile price and I pulled it off the market. "I will try again later," I thought, not realizing that my removal of the "For Sale "sign had another effect.

A good friend of mine, Doug, who had been helping with my building projects as a high school kid several years ago, returned to the neighborhood recently, unbeknownst to me, and he noticed the sign, "What? Trudy is selling, why?" When it disappeared, my friend became worried and knocked at the door to find out where I had moved to. We hadn't seen each other for several years. And now looking back, I know that there was another reason for the sign besides selling, one that would lead into a new direction for each one of us.

67. Joseph, the Carpenter's Hand

One of the decisions we had come to was for "Joseph", my friend Doug, to move into my house and dry out and turn his life around. I was just about to leave for Germany for Mother's 90th birthday, which turned out to be the last time I saw her. I suggested that my friend make himself feel at home, while I was gone and I offered him a tape of Chuck Swindoll, called "Joseph", because I didn't think he would be in a mood for reading. Not realizing how much that tape met his needs and ministered to his heart and how the solitude gave him an entirely new perspective. Something that our *God-of-the-Splitsecond* had in His gracious providence long before.

When I returned, I found a new man, with new hope, a new job and a new outlook, thanks also to pastoral counseling. With the inner restoration, he began to have new energy for the physical environment. I never expected that he should work on my house to correct some of the faults of my do-it-yourself renovations. But it also had another effect on him, it helped him to aleviate the desire to drink, and gave him new energy to work. He went through my house, tearing down damaged sheetrock, fixing windows, insulating. For me it was the gift of a completely restored living room by a "master builder", who knew what he was doing to correct the flaws in the room, which impeded my sale. Of course, I paid for the materials and labor too.

The greatest gift of all was a brand-new kitchen which my friend Doug installed perfectly, not just to bring my kitchen up to par with the upstairs apartment, but to make life easier and more hospitable. But when I think of my mother, who fed a large family and grandchildren in a small turn-around kitchen, I feel like a spoiled materialist.

This building activity went on for a year. One day, I went downstairs and found "Joseph" up to his ankles in flood water in my basement. There had always been water after a heavy rain or the melting of snow, and I had to vacuum it out and dump the water into the washing machine, and the sump pump hole, which was a hassle. After every incident I counted about 50 buckets a rainfall.

Bucket Brigade Formula. It amounts to a lot of heavy work. And it adds up like this: 50 buckets x 30 years = 1500 buckets, what a backache! There were more headache projects around the house, but this is not a worklog, but a family history book. However, we did apply the Episcopal prayer often: "Forgive us for the things done, and for the things left undone."

And since then the Carpenter Joseph was exchanging his tools for physical work with those of the mind. He is studying at college and keeping a strict schedule of work and study, as he is preparing for a career in computer design and programming.

Another part of this young man's life has been the beckoning call of the SEA, not as a lonely voyager on a boat sailing off to some distant shore, but rather in service to his country on a large airplane carrier with the Navy. The challenges and discipline of that assignment tell a different story. To work and live on such a large sea-going vessel is like being in a city on water.

One of his duties was being *"Mate of the Watch"*. He had to supervise the monitoring of gauges and controls which were vital to the life and survival of the carrier and its men. Several Navy men were assigned to monitor certain instruments throughout the ship to watch that they worked right.

Mate of the Watch... It echoes in my heart the task given to us on the Sea of Life. Not only are we as passengers of the ship which is the Church assigned tasks and duties for the welfare of that body. We also need to keep an alert eye and keep the Light shining brightly for those on the sin-tossed sea, seeking a safe harbor.

Panorama 1996

The year 1996 was rather unusual for me, not only because I was pouring over books and rummaging in libraries to prepare myself for the assignment in Kiev. It was also unusual in the visits I had, one of them being my oldest German nephew coming to the USA for the first time. One of my sisters brought a video of a documentary film showing the town we lived in during World War II. These pictures and a diary were rescued by two young Jews who escaped before the holocaust. Events in 1996 seemed like a beam of light shining on different epochs of my life, all coming together, or like the beautiful splendor of autumn reflected in the brilliant colors of a New England Maple. I can see each decade in the events of that year:

1933 **My trip to Kiev in the Ukraine**, or the first time since 60 years to my birthplace Theodorshof in Galizia.

1945 Seeing the **documentary film** "Hohenstein" about my hometown Poddembice and reviewing that time and place after 50 years on my TV.

1956 **meeting Elisabeth Elliot in Boston**, my college days in Canada at Toronto Bible College (now Tyndale College) 40 years ago, and the impact of the Auca missionaries in 1956 on students and the world.

1961 **GLORIA Hohner** – the accordion, and my youth ministry in Germany. This instrument had been sent to Kiev on a 2nd assignment.

1985 **my book "Morrow Sojourners",** putting it all together for my husband's Australian family whom I have never met, in a family book on the life and ministry of a pastor.

1995 **Babushka and the Accordion** – based on that dramatic event in Galizia (Poland) 50 years after our exodus to the West in 1945. And my assignment to lecture in Kiev, resulting in work to complete my manuscript on Apologetics for Teens *(and back to Kiev above)*.

68. Leipzig and the Candlelight Revolution

In the fall of 1994, I was able to make my first visit to what was once East Germany, the land behind the Iron Curtain, where Germans lived under Soviet-Communist dictatorship for 44 years. Even if I would dare to set foot on that land years earlier, I could have been confiscated and shipped to Siberia. The Soviets considered anybody born in their territory as their permanent subject! Now since the Berlin Wall had come tumbling down on November 9, 1989, it was safe to visit that territory.

With great anticipation I traveled to Leipzig, the city where Johann Sebastian Bach played his compositions on the organ of the famous St. Thomaskirche. I stepped inside and was impressed with the stark simplicity reflecting the great organ master's day. I saw the balcony from which his boys choir, known as "die Thomaner", presented their magnificent choral pieces. That choir still exists, only generations and generations later from those boys singing to the accompaniment of the Great Master.

Did you know, that there were 9 generations of Bach composers and musicians, ranging from the time of George Washington to Napoleon? There could have been a "Bach" entertaining for decades. The entire families and all the children devoted themselves to music.

Johann Sebastian Bach composed a new music piece for every Sunday, like the minister prepares his sermon. He is called the Fifth Gospeler. He loved the Lord and wanted to glorify Him. He signed his works with "In Jesu Namen" or "I.J.N." or he signed in Latin with "S.D.G." meaning "sole deo gloria." Today that is largely unknown and censored out by a biased culture.

I was taken to the glamorous plaza of Leipzig, which had gigantic frescos showing the glories of Bolshevism, Marx and Lenin, etc. (no longer applicable). And I walked the hundreds of steps up to the "Volksdenkmal", the peoples monument, a humongous structure with Roman flair, once used by the "Third Reich" and then by the Communists. I couldn't help but think of our own Lincoln Monument still standing, looking down to the Capitol Dome – still here.

Downtown we entered the "Nikolaikirche", the church where the Candlelight Revolution had its historic moment by an accidental spark that carried the flame of freedom. But I was ignorant of the actual events and the real story behind the news blimps. So I listened to my friends who were here on that day, recalling the scene in this very sanctuary in October 1989 (see the book by Bultmann). They related how the Gestapo surrounded the building with army trucks and were ready to shoot a group of people who had come peacefully to pray for peace and freedom. Monday was known to those people as the candle day anybody would come with a candle in his/her pocket or purse and light it carefully in solemn prayer as a symbol of hope.

I also learned that on that particular day rumor had spread among the Communists (and there was no such decision) that the peaceniks were going to revolt (but with candles?) So the Communists were told to get to the Nikolaikirche early and fill up any seat to keep those others out. When the candle people came to their usual Monday worship, there was no more room inside. Others were in that packed church, but you couldn't tell who is who. Then someone outside suggested, that they just walk along the streets with their candles, and you need to read the rest, there is so much to it.

But to think that confusion, not a general with an army started the Revolution. Or can you think of anything else? It reminds me of the Walls of Jericho and how ridiculous the defenseless, quiet mob of Israelites must have looked. But they had a great God in charge.

House Arrest for 50 Years.

My main reason to visit Leipzig was NOT to tour the city, but to see a special friend and her family after 50 years. Let me tell you another story. You know what it is for a child to be grounded for bad behavior and having your privileges taken away – no TV, no treat, no friends etc. But imagine being confined or grounded for 50 years. If you can't believe it, it happened to two girls who were good friends at school.

These two friends were one day rudely separated, not by their parents, but by the cruel actions of a cruel ruler, Stalin.

As their parents fled from their hometown, one family ended up in the free West Germany, the other in the Soviet zone of East Germany. And they lost touch with each other until a few years later. The young girls started writing letters to each other, but that was soon stopped, because the girl in the Soviet zone was told by the government that she will be expelled from school, not allowed to attend university and her parents will lose their job, if they continue their contact with those dangerous West Germans. Mind you, simple letter writing between teenagers? And that marked the beginning of the house arrest.

I had often wondered about my school friend Nehta, but was unable to establish contact with her, she had married, changed names and locations. Until in 1994 I learned of her living in Leipzig. So my sister Ilse and I drove in her little Volkswagen along the highways, and it was my first visit beyond the once known Iron Curtain, seeing the incarcerated "Volksnachbarn" and how they lived. Even five years after the collapse of the Berlin Wall you could see drastic evidence of poverty and neglect of a nation that had put all efforts into guns, and hardly any into butter.

The highways between towns were new, courtesy of Westdeutschland. But when you entered towns or villages, you puttered over cobblestone roads with big potholes, lined by rundown houses that never saw paint, windows and doors rotten to the core, buildings that could tell a sorrowful tale of neglect. Once in awhile you could see a brightly shining house fixed with new windows, clean paint, even a bit of landscaping. It stood out like a foreign object or a comet from heaven. What happened here? Some "Westerner" may have bought it and fixed it up, I was told, or maybe some "Easterner" with a good job in the West.

As we entered Leipzig, we were impressed with the many tall cranes reaching above the buildings, and we were told, that there were 100 construction cranes rebuilding junk buildings from scratch. Also that the entire telephone system of East Germany consisting of poor copper wire had to be redone by West Germany and that some of the larger companies could have bought the whole caboodle of a country. Wow!

My sister and I were heading for the apartment of my school friend, herself a grandmother by now. We recalled childhood memories and exchanged many stories to catch up on each other's lives. It was great to see her grown children and the little ones. No, I didn't have to go through trials and tribulations as they had. I have become a fortunate American with so many blessings and opportunities in this great land. I wonder how I would have stood the test of fire as they and thousands of others did. One evening we were invited to speak at the church meeting, and I was asked to give my testimony. Looking into the eyes of those, who had endured so much suffering, I felt worthless. But they were such gracious people and it was a blessing to be near those overcomers.

Since this was the day in September, when high school kids would meet around the pole to pray, I gave a message with these thoughts:

69. See you at the Pole!

"While I am here in Leipzig, meeting with my school friend after 50 years of separation, there is a special event taking place all over the United States, boys and girls in high schools joining hands with each other around the flag pole and praying. It's called "See you at the Pole". I am too old for that, but I have stood around a few poles myself."

And now I want to give you the gist of my message, it may be a bit lengthy, but it relates to the experiences in this book:

The May Pole: As a little girl I watched the young people dance around that pole in our village in Eastern Europe. Somebody had climbed up to the top and fastened dozens of colorful ribbons that reached to the ground for the dancers to hold on to. They were rejoicing that spring had finally come, time to sow, plant, work, enjoy life. I hopped along not knowing much, but being happy.

Then one day in 1939 tragedy hit our village. We were forced by a Nazi squad to leave our peaceful home, packed into trains and shipped to Poland to live in an empty house, whose owners were sent into some labor camp.

The Nazi Pole: I was made to stand at this pole as a school-girl wearing uniform. I remember one day we marched to the town square to join a full plaza and watch some Jews being hanged. I was so shocked, because I had never seen horror or violence that you might see on TV today in America. I was made to pay homage to that system as a child of the "New Age" which was to last 1000 years. But that pole came down sooner.

The Communist Pole: This is the one I escaped from because of the vision and courage of my father. You see, after World War II there was only a 2-week period in 1945 for a "legitimate exchange" of refugees who ended up in the Russian zone while escaping from the Allies. My father saw this as our golden opportunity to slip away into the West, as we walked through Checkpoint "Soviet", before they put up mine fields and fences.

But I know someone who had to live under this pole, my school buddy from Leipzig. She and others who had to listen, recite, think, act out what socialism dictated to them. They had to give up any contact with the West for 44 years until the wall came down eventually. I am glad to be here today and visit with my friend's family and with you.

Did you know that these people behind the Iron Curtain had an **Invisible Pole**? One, whose obscure location they secretly passed on to trusted friends or fellow-sufferers; the road map was handed out in sections (like a treasure hunt), you only knew the next stop to the place of worship, maybe a deserted building or the middle of woods. It reminds me of the Underground Railroad of the slaves in America. How history repeats itself.

The Christian Pole: I don't mean the one that stands in our sanctuary near the pulpit or altar (you only see that in America, I think). Woops, I remember, we did have a flag in our churches too – the Nazi flag which was usually carried in before the service by some soldier of the Reich. We just whispered among ourselves, "Vorsicht, Feind hört mit!" (Beware, enemy is listening!)

The Solidarity Pole: No, I am thinking of another pole in Poland, when about 500 school children marched to the town square holding a crucifix in their raised hands, shouting, "We want the cross on our classroom wall again!" You see, it was just one element of the brave SOLIDARITY movement that eventually brought them freedom from Communism.

And then I can't forget the pole in Tiananmen Square in Beijing, Taiwan (which has since become part of China), where about 100,000 students and protestors gathered around the age-old unceasing cry of the human heart, inspired by our American idea of Liberty. The army moved in and shot about 3000 of these demonstrators.

There have been and still are many poles like those all over the world.

The New Age Pole: That is a subtle one that is cropping up here and there, trying to replace other poles – or combining all of them under the caption of "change". The new name shouldn't fool you, its idea is ancient. What is new in America, though, is that it claims exclusive right to exist under American "pluralism". While setting up a pretty high fence by the myth of "separation of church and state" and a threatening thought-police pushing "political correctness".

The recent 40 year anniversary of the gathering of 200,000 young people at the muddy "pole" meadow in Woodstock, New York, back in 1968 tells the story of secular humanism as does the social malaise of drugs, sex and violence of the last 50 years. Under the elusive claim of <u>not</u> being a religion, a host of things have spawned under this pole that are just that. Enter your psychic friends, the Satanists, the occult, the Rock Crusaders, as well as TM Channeling & Company.

So why have you been thrown out by the tolerant crowd in our "pluralistic" America just because you are a Christian? Seems like they have set up a "state church" for themselves, the very thing our forefathers wanted to protect us from – by giving us the Bill of Rights. By now it's time to join your brave friends at

The American Pole: That's the pole that I like best of all. It used to be a good one, a cherished place of courage and hope, where *"We The People"* gathered in the land of liberty and justice for all. You got it right, you are standing there as an American, as a citizen who just happens to be a Christian – or a cultural conservative, or whatever your conviction and belief.

You may think you are just a handful of kids on your local school lawn. No, in July 1994 there were 200,000 of you by proxy (3x5 cards signed by teenagers) which 20,000 teens placed on mall lawn facing the Washington Capitol. And there are more of you all over the land. The message on these proxy cards and those representing them was on chastity and virtue "Love Can Wait".

The Post-Modern Pole: Today in the new Millennium 2000 I could add another pole, the one the Existentialists from the 60s culture erected for themselves. It means you are living in your own subjective world today with no reference to eternal truths and realities. That shaky pole has been embraced by the Post-Mods. "There is no Truth, and everything is meaningless." So evil isn't evil, if you are a nice person. Be nice and don't antagonize anyone, even a killer.

The problem seems to be that people do no longer distinguish between ideas and persons. I may like a person very much, but I may not necessarily agree with his or her ideas. We have been told that "political correctness" is being nice and accepting the other person's view without making any judgment.

And thus we close the door to any dialogue or rational discussion about any issue. Instead we are expected to feel insulted or misunderstood, when in reality there are different views and beliefs. What we are deprived of doing is a logical comparison of issues and making a non-threatening conclusion. Somehow I think that the term "political correctness" can also mean "personal cowardice" or "prescribed coersion". There is such a thing as objective truth.

70. Yale Shadow

Ever since my husband-to-be chose New Haven as his intellectual home base, we have been living within the range of that famous, magnificent gothic place know as Yale University. Denis studied at the Berkeley Divinity School in preparation for the priesthood in the Episcopal Church and lived on the campus during his bachelor years. Later we rented an apartment within walking distance of the Peabody Natural Museum. We admired the giant dinosaurs, many of those fossils were discovered in Connecticut, although we always questioned the rigid arguments of Evolutionists who used these finds as unshakeable evidence for their case.

Philip Johnson, a lawyer, said in one of his books that it takes more faith to believe in the origin of life by chance and in those presumed millions of years of random evolution than to believe in an intelligent Creator, and so Johnson switched.

We remember the years in the '60s, when the Black Panthers and the SDS gathered on the New Haven Green and Yale Chaplain Sloan Coffin made his liberating speeches, and when Woodstock, NY, left the mark on the giant rain-and-mud sex party on the fields, but also in the minds of misguided liberated youths.

Personally I enjoyed the aesthetic and architectural splendor of Yale, it was like walking through a little bit of Europe, maybe Oxford or some other place of antiquity. At that time, students did not carry handguns, condoms, cellular phones, or ID-cards which they press into a slot in the entrance door of their dormitory or fraternity.

We as outsiders living in an apartment could meander in and out of the various colleges. No longer! Yale has become an electronic fortress. We used to step into a cafeteria in the evening and join the line for a snack or an easy supper. Each of the colleges is built inside a square street block and has its own courtyard in the middle. On Friday nights we used to sit in the balcony of the Music Hall and enjoy the rehearsals of soloists or choirs, such as the men's choir "the Wiffenpoofs" – I love that name. Or we would listen to the Slavic Choir. We would go to hear a pianist or orchestra in the large Woolsey Hall. In fact, we picked many of the campus events from our own copy of the Yale-Bulletin.

No more. The Ivory Tower has become a forbidden place. One of our favorite spots was the big Sterling Library. The Main Hall is built like a tall cathedral and thousands of card indexes are arranged in the catacomb arches, now having been replaced by a computer database We browsed and milled around the new underground library which is hidden underneath a luscious lawn above, where students walk or play Frisbee, etc. while others study below. Such a smart and noble effort of Yale to save the open space of the Green. We would explore the Beinecke Library and admire the original books and manuscripts, among them one of the Gutenberg Presses and an original printed Bible. Also, the diaries of Governor Bradford and the Puritans.

The Yale Divinity campus near the Winchester Firearms Company has an interesting layout with arching walkways on both sides of the lawn. It reminded me of some of the old cloisters in Europe. We'd hear organ concerts or practices of students. Denis lived in the school nearby across from the gymnastics hall nicknamed the "Yale Whale". At that time I felt somewhat out-of-place at Berkeley among seminarians robed in long black gowns, the traditional academic attire. No one thought or dared to "dress down" in tight jeans and sneakers back then.

Change About Face

If my husband were alive today, he would not recognize Yale anymore. This famous place was founded by Puritans as one of the first universities in the New World and had its beginning days in the little "Academy" on the Green in Branford in one little building.

Peter Marshall, a Yale graduate, elaborates in his book "From Sea to Shining Sea" on the tremendous influence and greatness of men like Timothy Dwight, President of Yale, and others like John Davenport, John Winthrop, etc. This one-time mecca of academia has turned more into a political breeding ground for liberalism and post-mod confusion. Whenever I stroll through the campus, I find little academic items on the bulletin boards, but plenty of radical heat. Maybe the real agenda and information is found on the student's laptop computers.

What my husband would have abhorred is the degradation of moral standards of the campus maybe since feminism made its inroads and the ACLU fought for equality in male colleges. I don't object to Yale being a co-ed university now but rather on their arrangement of their co-ed dormitories.

Worst of all, and the biggest scandal are the co-ed bathrooms and shower stalls apparently with no curtains in place. Imagine a young maiden from the Midwest (or any well-bred home environment) showering herself and a young stud passing by the scene? You don't even have this kind of intrusion of privacy in our homes, where family members or visitors lock themselves in for a bath or a brief visit. Why is it ok with strangers? What a disgrace!

But the intellectual scene of the ivory league college has changed as well and become more of a brainwashing hotbed under the concept of "political correctness". At a place that should be the innovative, free breeding ground for inquiry and logical formulation of ideas. Instead, it has become a crippling and intimidating sphere of meaningless misdirected so-called tolerance, the mind ordered to regress into irrationalism, because one vital essence of truth is missing.

ALL MUSHROOMS ARE EQUAL,
ALL MUSHROOMS ARE EQUAL.

All truth is God's truth, however, when man barricades himself into his own eclectic world – anything but sub-truths and irrelevance can come out of it. Thus is the judgment of secularism and humanism. But where are the lightbearers?

71. Nudus Modus Yalenum

I had just woken up from dream and in my slumbering stupor, I tried to make sense of a scene which seemed so real. But before this anatomical event would drift into cranial oblivion, my mind captured one word "nudus" – nudus what?

What bothered me more than the plot was WHY did I dream this dream? Had I eaten something that caused this nightmare or did I read something related to the plot to produce such unusual scene? No, my day was spent in hard work on the computers, plotting figures and budgets. I read a delightful story just before I fell asleep, nothing like the event in my dream:

Dressed in an appropriate classy suit and armed with notes and a briefcase, I found myself in a one-day seminar at Yale University together with a group of students from various places and countries. We sat in a circle discussing the topic which I can't remember, but I can see myself participating in the dialog and I felt confident in my own contribution. I recall that we dispersed into various adjoining rooms and then gathered for a final wrap-up.

Not until then did I notice that I was in an unusual academic environment, because I had been preoccupied with the intellectual atmosphere of this famous place. As individuals from this or that side of the room were expressing their opinions or leafing though their notebooks on their lap (laptop computers had not been invented yet), I noticed that they were stark naked. And suddenly I looked out of place in my dress suit. I also noticed Bill Clinton in this group, moving in and out among the students as one of them, also in the same "sans" attire.

What an odd dream! Something else must have bothered my subconscience to produce this, and now I know why, we just heard about the news about the Monica Lewinski episodes and our illustrious President Clinton, who is a Yale graduate.

Three Men in the Fiery Furnace

I am sure you remember the story in the Book of Daniel, where three brave Jewish men, Shadrech, Mesach and Obendigo, challenged the emperor and refused to bow down and worship him. They were indeed heroes of faith.

Somehow what happened at Yale in 1998, reminded me of that story. Here were some young orthodox Jewish students, who were qualified and accepted to study at Yale. But the requirements are that Freshmen live on campus during the first year. However these three students protested on the grounds that it was detrimental to their religion, that they could not live in the immoral environment of co-ed dorms. They asked for a refund of the boarding fees so that they could live outside or stay with parents in town.

As you know, Yale was adamant and refused to give in, so these students filed a lawsuit against the university. It made national news, but eventually they lost, because, I am afraid, not too many stood with them to support them in their noble fight. It reminded me of what Niebuhr said during the WWII: "First it was the Jews, but I did not come to their aid because I was not a Jew. Then it was the Catholics, but I did not help them because I was not a Catholic. Then it was the Protestants, but nobody was there to help me now."

Iron Curtain of the Mind

I browse through the Yale-Coop and Bookstore occasionally to read titles, also in the philosophy and religion section, just as I do regularly at Barnes & Noble. Regardless of any of these stores, what is effectively censored out of existence are leading books from the evangelical scene and many other well-known authors. What you find in their section of "religion" are ancient, obscure titles or a few token books by Billy Graham, Joyce Meyers and other lesser authors for good measure.

When I asked the manager, if they had a section on conservatism, which is not even a religious term, I was told that they can't do that, because they would have to categorize all others (whatever he meant by that). My reply, "but you have a whole section on New Age and Spiritualism (occult)." I got an embarrassed shrug from the manager.

One day I went to the Yale Divinity Bookstore and browsed through all the sections to see what titles they carried. I noticed a large section on feminism and mythology, the occult etc., but was unable to find even one book of our leading authors. I inquired at the desk about Francis Schaeffer or Charles Swindoll and was told, "We don't keep these books in our store. Only if the professor makes them a reading requirement for his students."

When I asked, "but how can these students know what the arguments of conservatives or evangelicals are, if they can't read their books or go to original sources?" A puzzled look by the manager, obviously we have censorship even in the religious part of Yale. I feel not only part of a subculture, but of an anti-intellectual ghetto. I suppose, we must become effective communicators and apologists of our worldview which is often censored out of the marketplace of ideas. I am glad that men like Colson, Sproul, Zacharias an others present such clear, rational message of our worldview and faith.

Boa Constrictor on the Broadway Blvd

Occasionally I made a trip to the Yale bookstores on my lunch time. As I walked on the sidewalk on a sunny August day, I heard a male voice behind me saying: "Oh, look out!" I noticed that I had stepped onto something soft and thought, "too late, it must be dog dirt. How nice of him to warn me!"

But as I looked down, I saw a big snake slizzering away from me, whose head I must have touched or barely brushed with my shoe. It was about 6-foot long and had a big belly. I panicked, thinking the critter is now angry and will strike. Other pedestrians stopped and looked, and a business man in a smart suit approached and just shook his head.

I looked at the young man behind me in a colorful hippy outfit and his purple hair was sticking up in Afro-fashion. So I restrained myself and only said, "why do you have your snake here? You shouldn't do this, it's dangerous." But he smiled as he picked up his snake and dropped it on the sidewalk again a few feet behind me. I wondered if another pedestrian might have the same frightening experience or even get a heart attack.

Browsing through the Yale record store took my mind off from that traumatic experience. On my way to the car, I saw a policeman, waved to him and reported that Boa incident. He didn't seem to be impressed. "Sir I am making a verbal complaint. This could frighten customers away from the Boulevard. I could have had a heart attack!" He didn't answer. I hurried back to my office still upset about the incident and phoned the restaurant "Educated Burgher" at that location. "Yes, he comes to our restaurant some time." Again, apathy from the voice on the phone. "Who would like to eat there when a guy with a boa draped around his neck enters?" I said and hung up the phone wondering how people can confuse a pet with a threat. How things have changed in this confused world of ours.

72. Age of Dot.Com and the Y2K Panic

Since the computer has become a household word and an indispensable tool, the electronic miracle has changed our lives. I remember the time, when IBM and Honeywell were the only two companies making computers, but they were the size of a room. Instead of floppies, zip files or CD Rom and stick drives, information was filed on large reels like the ancient film rolls in metal containers. And whatever IBM, the No.1 company printed out, appeared on "punch cards", a piece of card stock that was full of mysterious holes or chads, like Morse codes.

But with hi-tech and the discovery of the Internet, our lives have been thrust into cyberspace. Once the sole property of the government, now anybody can have a piece of the pie. He or she can even have her own website. I have wondered sometime if the thing will not get out of hand and the globe will collapse from the sheer weight of this?

As we anticipated the turn of the century and the dawn of a new millennium, the threat of a global meltdown caused by a computer glitch, namely the difficulty to absorb and read the new dates starting with 2000 caused concern. This pending doom was known as "Y2K". Companies and the government spent great sums of money to prepare their computers for this potential blackout and wipeout of data. How would you be able to claim your insurance, verify your birthday, get your pension, secure your document – if there was nothing in the computer databanks left to verify?

Strangely enough, we survived that transition without any catastrophe, and people asked "What happened?" or should we say, "What didn't happen?"

73. Millennium Cathedral

For a person's lifespan to encompass two millennia is a rare experience. My grandmother Elizabeth (mother's side) was born in the year 1888 and lived to be 92 years of age. She too had a wide span of life experience from our original colony in Galizia, Eastern Europe, where her ancestors from the Black Forest in Germany settled in 1782 to the deportation by Hitler in 1939, and eventually her immigration to Toronto Canada to live there with her daughters.

But I also lived through two centuries and welcomed the year 2000 here in New England. We escaped the much feared Y2K crisis, it never happened.

Eventually I ran across the concept and checked things out on the Internet. There are a couple of Millennium Cathedrals in England, but they are basically some dedicated new wing of an existing cathedral or some impressive new stained glass window. London even has a unique modern Millennium Bridge. I wanted to create a board game with this idea, but I soon discovered that it was too difficult to have it printed and sold.

74. September 11 and The Aftermath

Who in the world does NOT remember 9-11 and the horror on that fateful Tuesday in 2001? My boss passed my desk and said, "Good morning! They have just struck the Twin Towers." My mind did not register, because I was preoccupied with my work. Only a few minutes later as I walked to our clinic to get a freshly brewed cup of coffee, did I notice people starring at the television suspended from the ceiling. In fact, as we looked, the announcer said, "Oh, I think another plane just flew into the second Tower."

And a third plane was diverted from its ultimate goal and crashed in some wooded area, only because someone was brave – with the heart of a hero and the faith of a true Christian. **Ron Beamer**, while talking to his wife on the phone, heard that a plane had crashed into the Tower in New York. The highjackers told them, that if the passengers wanted to make some last phone calls, they could. Ron Beamer could have spent the time in self-pity that he would not see his wife and children again. Instead he thought of others and the possible target.

Quickly he conspired with the other passengers to overtake the highjackers and cause the plane to come down instantly. On the signal **"Let's Roll"** they moved into action.

There is no room to tell the entire story of the somewhat 4000 people who died in the Twin Towers. What a tragedy, but there are many stories of miraculous escape of some and the brave rescue that many firemen and others provided while risking their own lives.

It was a wakeup call for America! There were spontaneous prayer vigils and gatherings. In our little town about 500 people met on the football park to pray and sing "God bless America!" But only if we are consistent with our cry for help and trust Him.

"If my people who are called by my name, will humble themselves, and pray and turn from their wicked ways: then I will hear from heaven, and will forgive their sin, and will heal their land." 2. Chron. 2:14

75. Ich bin ein Neu-Engländer
When President Kennedy stood on the scaffold in West Berlin overlooking the Brandenburg Gate behind the impregnable Berlin Wall, he said those impressive words "Ich bin ein Berliner!" ("ein" pronounced like "ine") which had significant meaning for the divided country.

My own little phrase is especially said to my family in Germany, because I feel very much at home in New England and have spent more of my life – over 40 years on this Connecticut shoreline. I would not have chosen to come to the United States on my own back in 1967, I was a Canadian by that time, and the US was too big and too troublesome for me with the riots and upheaval going on. But I met a young Australian student in Toronto who had his sights set for New York or New England. When he proposed to me he said that he found a city where I would feel at home. By saying yes to him, I had to make a double decision for a man and a country.

I love New England, I have spent here more years than anywhere else. It is my home. As a one-time landlubber, I love the ocean, the vast expanse of hills and mountains, as well as the farms and those quaint towns, many of them are preserved with the historic architecture and clapboard houses. In the summer, this area is visited by tourists from many places. I don't care if there is a California, Florida, Texas or even the Rocky Mountains in this great country from sea to shining sea. I belong here to NE.

Recently I added a lovely porch to the back of my house overlooking the garden as a spot for relaxation, instead of the couch and TV which I got rid of while I worked in the office. I wanted to carve out more time in the evening and spend it at my Mac computer writing in the sunset of my life.

This land is my land as an immigrant and a New American and because I have come to understand the unique beginning of America's history as a nation with a great Christian heritage.

One Nation Under God, Indivisible, With Liberty and Justice for All.

76. Götterdämmerung

Another German word, meaning "twilight of the gods" which implies the decline of divine gods and the coming apocalypse or whatever danger in which we find ourselves in. Perhaps more appropriately it could refer to societal corruption.

Somehow I can't help but believe that we are in such a period, inspite of all our admirable ingenious technology and science. The "gods" or idols or treasures we worshipped seem to fail us, or they fade away. Whatever took the place of the One True God Jehovah, who never changes or fades away, is no great help in our need at the time. And this troublesome condition is evident practically in the whole world.

In fact, we have managed to surround ourselves with busyness (yes) and constant noise and stress that we never get time and quiet to THINK about ourselves. We can't shop without that constant background music, or be in any public place without drowning our thoughts and let us have peace and solitude. We have become a "flat society", only living in the moment and our earthly endeavors. But we have a spiritual dimension as well. Someone said, we are not bodies with a soul, but rather a soul clothed in a body.

The world is too much with us, each one must carefully tend to his or her own purpose of life while at the same time seeking to serve others.

Part IV

God's Miracles in Other Lives

*T*hese stories stood out in some of the literature I read, where I saw that others had "God-of-the-Splitsecond" experiences too. Squanto, the Cape Cod Indian, and his 15-year preparation before meeting the Pilgrims at Plymouth, impressed me.

The most dramatic and gigantic action of God I learned about recently, but it happened in 1947 in Berlin in the amazing escape of more than one thousand Mennonites in a freight train to get to a waiting ship which would take them to freedom in Paraguay. They call this epic event "Exodus through the Red Sea". The miracle was that they made it through the tight surveillance in the Soviet zone without being noticed. God blinding the enemy?

Francis Schaeffer's L'Abri with its daring enterprise of faith like George Müller, and the many seekers and wanderers finding hope and faith at the L'Abri shelter high in the Swiss Alps.

I couldn't decide which stories to leave out, so I selected a few from World War II, other momentous events in history, and some from the American scene.

I hope you don't get the impression from this book that the sensational should define one's life. We walk by faith, not by sight, these GDS-events are just highlights, stars on my horizon. Our character is proven in the drudgery and challenges of living in the humdrum world that rejects and ignores the Lord of life.

77. Berlin Exodus Through The Red Sea

Leafing through a book recently which a friend gave me, I discovered a story of a mighty work of God's deliverance that happened in Germany in 1947, about sixty five years ago. Just as the Pilgrims experienced God's protection and guidance in America in 1620, so these 1200 refugees from Russia saw the hand of God lead them to freedom in 1947 and to a new homeland in Paraguay, South America.

This epic event is recorded in the American War Records of World War II and is not a fabricated fairytale. As the drama unfolds on the pages of the book "Up From The Rubble" by Peter and Elfrieda Dyck depicting the heroic pilgrimage of the suffering of those Mennonites, I could see the people of my homeland in the Ukraine, whose fate was similar. But before I describe that miraculous "Berlin Exodus", I need to paint a picture of the background to this drama. Otherwise it will read like a flat news report and the reader will merely follow the event of an unusual train ride and miss the whole point. Let me recapture the "why" and "how" from the pages of the book.

RUSSIAN MENNONITES.

One by one they came, or in fragmented families, some of their loved ones had been tortured and died. Some had been taken to Gulag prisons or were shipped to Siberia. The ravages of Stalin and the persecution, torture and famine forced them to escape to Western Europe. But it was a long treacherous ordeal through woods, rivers, in the darkness of night. Hungry and frightened fugitives they were, hiding in ditches and barns from the lurking threat of their Soviet captors, who would drag them back to a living hell.

If they could only make it to the land of their ancestors - Holland, they would be safe! Then perhaps they could get a ship to America, the land of ultimate freedom? They would be an ocean away from danger. The oppression and cruelty in their "Egypt" and the ray of hope of "Canaan" gave them strength to carry on at any cost. At one time they thought they were being liberated from the Soviets by the invading German army in 1941, only to discover that their hope was short-lived. In the fall of 1943 as the Nazi army retreated, Mennonite communities left their villages and moved along with them to settle in East Germany. They loaded some meager possessions on horse-drawn covered wagons to make an arduous journey of 1200 km. Children, old people and the weak were loaded onto freight trains - destination occupied Poland. But the picture changed and with the collapse of Germany, these fugitives had to resume their flight westward.

It must have been a harrowing experience for these peace-loving Christian communities. One group of 614 people ended up with only 33 people of survivors! Many died, most of them were eventually confiscated and forcefully returned to the Soviet Union. From the 35,000 Mennonites who fled to Western Europe, 21,000 were either kidnapped by the KGB in Yugoslavia, Austria, Germany or elsewhere, and "repatriated" i.e. sent back to the Soviet countries.

MOTHER HOLLAND
Some Mennonite refugees were fortunate enough to make it to Holland from where their ancestors had left about 500 years ago. But Holland herself was a starved, ravaged nation, a victim of Nazi oppression. And the Soviets soon

plugged up that hole of escape. Others were able to land in the Allied Occupation Zone of Germany (the American, French or British zones). Thus, the refugees who in 1946 made it to the American Sector of the City of Berlin, an isle of hope, which was surrounded by the "Red Sea" of the Soviets. You may remember Berlin was divided into four occupation zones like a piece of pie.

The Dutch part of this story is another amazing chapter by itself. It was there, that the authors of the book "Up from the Rubble" Peter and Elfrieda Dyck helped the Dutch people with many shipments of food and clothing provided by the humanitarian aid of Mennonites in Canada and the USA. In fact, about 10,000 people had starved to death under the Nazis. Now they were being rejuvenated, as one out of four Dutchmen received aid from the MCC – Mennonite Central Committee. But the doors were closing and there were streams of Mennonite refugees stuck in Germany.

CAMP LIFE IN BERLIN

They made it through the rubble and ruins of the demolished city, hiding in deserted places of the city. These Christian believers were an unusual group whose suffering and faith forged them into one loving colony - like one big family. While Berlin was still in ruins, there was chaos, food was scarce, these Mennonites survived on a meager subsistence. They disciplined themselves and willingly helped in all the chores at their camp, the kitchen, the children's work and school and the makeshift hospital. About 1000 people tucked away in nine houses, like sardines, as blankets partitioned off the cramped bunk bedrooms. The young couple, Peter and Elfrieda Dyck, sent from the Mennonite Central Committee in Canada to lead this work with no previous experience of that kind. They were marvelously used by the Lord in this adventure, as they had to look to him for that "Pillar of Fire" for the next step. Imagine the creativity of those people, when they found some old checkbooks in the ruins and used these as notebooks for 600 students in the camp school. Pencils were obtained from the American GI store. But they had no textbooks or anything else needed in a school, but enough good teacher volunteers for the job, and each class met daily in a designated area of the camp. In fact, it was their dedication and care for each other, which made them survivors even in the cruel uninhabitable Chaco of Paraguay where other settlers before them had failed. That's why this story is so fascinating. God leading His people through a 20th century wilderness.

What would you do for a Christmas program for the children if there were no stores to buy toys? You'd make them, but with what? Elfrieda's ingenious ideas and those of the women using scraps and sugar bags with floral prints to make dolls, aprons etc. The men whittling away at planes and other things to thrill a boy's heart. The Mennonites in Canada and USA followed the plight of their fellow-believers with great interest and sacrificial material help. Food and clothing was sent via Holland to them by some empty Dutch Red Cross trucks en route to Berlin to pick up their Dutch refugees. These trucks brought some of the food, sugar, flower, raisins, dehydrated potatoes, etc. to the camp.

And they saved some of this food for an unusual "cookie baking campaign". Peter talked to a local baker to let them use his ovens, tables and utensils from midnight till morning for two weeks. Elfrieda asked whether the women would like to mix dough for cookies and peppernuts (gingerbread) for Christmas. They were so excited and organized themselves into teams to mix dough, bake or cut cookies. Peter and Elfrieda would set the alarm clock to 2:00 am to visit these baking brigades and see how they were doing. For Christmas, there was a bag of cookies for everyone. A real Christmas tree decorated with paper stars and garlands. Each child received a little handmade gift and some cookies. They also invited Colonel Stinson, the person from the American Army in charge of refugees in their territory, to share Christmas joy with them.

One Sunday, the Mennonites had a communion service in the old gym nearby. There were no chairs so they all stood, except the needy ones would sit on a suitcase or makeshift box. They had no wine, but Coca Cola served as a sanctified means. No hymnbooks either, the songs they sang they all knew by heart, like "So nimm denn meine Hände und führe mich" (Take thou my hand and lead me). These people maintained their mother tongue of Plattdeutsch, a German-Dutch dialect. The hymns they carried in their heart was the only safe treasure that united them to their homeland, their ancestors and the worldwide church.

FROM WHENCE COMETH OUR HELP?

No, Berlin was no permanent stay for them. Peter Dyck and the MCC were working on highly secret plans to get these 1200 people out, but both the Canadian and the US government refused to take them as immigrants. Their only hope became South America. But how to get there - most ships had been destroyed during the war. Queen Juliana of Holland offered one of her ships, the "Volendam" to take the group from the West German port of Bremerhaven, if they could make it there. Colonel Stinson took their plight to heart and the American Army volunteered a military train to transport the 1200 Mennonites to that harbor. But it was so risky - should the Russians get wind that a whole train of Mennonite refugees is traveling through their zone, they could be sure that the trainload would be turned around and sent straight to Russia.

All the Mennonites in that Berlin camp knew that their leaders, Peter and Elfrieda and the MCC were working hard to get them out. Perhaps if Washington would give its stamp of approval, they would have powerful protection.

Perhaps they could be "lifted up" by Army planes to get to Bremerhaven? But it would take perhaps 25 planes. They didn't know that a few months later, all highways to Berlin would be cut off by the Soviet's attempt to strangle Berlin into subjection.

We know it as the "Berlin Air Lift", when 800 planes would drop food and other necessities in single day. This hunger war would last for a whole year. And so did the Allied effort to supply the Berliners day and night. You need to consider that in the ruined city there was no "Stop&Shop" or any other store for that matter. And did you hear the story of the "Chocolate Pilot" who had pity on the children and made little sweet parachutes out of handkerchiefs – with candy and chocolate?

THE SHIP AND THE GENERAL

One day, Peter Dyck was called to the Colonel's office who was obviously upset about something. Their plan to get the Mennonites out of Berlin was scrapped. By whom? Why? General Clay in charge of the Allied Forces thought the train idea was dangerous. That was a blow to Peter. Why now, when the ship had been hired and was waiting for them with 300 refugees from Holland already on board and 100 more from Munich on the way? For every day in the harbor, it cost them $15,000 extra.

Peter decided to go and see General Clay in person. His secretary asked him to fill out a form, but he learned that he would get a response in 10 days. Impossible, with the ship waiting? So Peter handed her the handwritten letter he prepared at home. Would she please give it to the General while he waited. That piece of paper with a divinely guided appeal became the instrument to change the course of action for the "Volendam", because the General did come out of his office and asked Peter Dyck to come in. So they discussed the situation to see what can be done. They decided to ask Washington for directions.

THE PRAYER MEETING

But the response from Washington was discouraging, i.e. it would be alright with them if the Russians agreed to it, which was like the cat telling the mouse that it's ok to come out. All plans failed, now Peter must tell the people who had their hopes up ready to leave for Paraguay. They didn't even know that the ship was waiting. Now, after 9 hopeful months they were stranded on the island of Berlin. With tears and sadness they prayed and pleaded the Most High for a miracle to happen. Then they went quietly to their bunk bed homes.

Peter had to dash off in his car to Bremerhaven to tell the passenger on the ship to go ahead, because the Berlin group would NOT be coming.

FAREWELL ON THE DECK

While the passengers were on the top deck for a farewell service on deck, Peter Dyck shared with J.C. Klassen and other MCC workers what the verdict was about Berlin. It was a sad moment. Suddenly two American MPs (military police) rushed up the plank and asked for Peter Dyck. "You have a telephone call on our Hot Line!" Hurriedly they ran down the plank, into their jeep to get to the nearby office, where the phone was off the hook. "Is the ship still there?" was the question to Peter by an unidentified caller. "Can you hold the ship?" "Why?" Peter asked puzzled to which came the clear answer: "Your Mennonite people in Berlin are cleared. Just hold the ship for them." And the caller hung up.

As Peter got back to the ship, he learned that the Captain also received a phone call to hold the ship indefinitely. But the passengers did not know what all this commotion was about. So Peter asked to use the intercom. "Quiet please, real quiet on the whole ship." "God is going to do a miracle.

The Berlin group is coming!" That's all he could say in this emotional moment. He also saw the reaction of the crowd of people on their faces. The ship became silent, nobody spoke, it was an awesome moment. Peter and two others rushed to his jeep to dash off back to Berlin. It would take them more than an hour to get there. As they stopped at the border in Helmstedt (between the British and the Russian zones) a British officer asked "Is one of you Dr. Dyck?" He had a message "the train is gone." Peter pretended not to know and asked "what train?" but the officer did not know more.

OPERATION MENNONITE

One could feel the sad and depressed mood everywhere, and the campers were freezing on this cold January day because they had been using up their coal in hopes of leaving soon. So Elfrieda Dyck called on the Displaced Person's office to ask for more coal. Colonel Stinson noticed her and called her into his office and asked: "Mrs. Dyck, just in case you could still go, how much time would you need to get ready?" Her reply: "Just give me an hour." The Colonel, an army man, must have been surprised to hear that she would have over a thousand civilians, old women, children and the sick ready in that short time.

That evening, the people got together for prayer. Having all hopes dashed, they looked to God for a miracle. One person put his small luggage outside the hallway, others followed. The ship was to leave the next day.

Stinson called and asked Elfrieda to stay in the apartment near the telephone. It was the longest day for her. At 3:40 pm the phone rang, it was General Clay's secretary, "Can I speak to Mr. Dyck?" She told her that he was in Bremerhaven. "I'll call you back, if I can't reach him." At about 6:00 pm the phone rang, "Can you come to headquarters immediately?" meaning Colonel Stinson's office. As she got there, he was discussing details with about 10 military officers. "Mrs.

Dyck, the Mennonites are leaving tonight. Be ready in an hour and a half. Have your people ready at 8:00 pm, standing outside their houses, Army trucks will pick them up and take them to the railroad station Lichterfelde-West. Have your men organize loading and unloading luggage. And please tell your people to be quiet, no talking on the street or to each other."

As Elfrieda hesitated for a minute before she slipped out of the office to hurry back with the good news, she overheard the Colonel giving orders to the officers and giving each specific responsibilities, food rations, even heaters. This was OPERATION MENNONITE, two things were important: speed and low profile and it was amazing that every detail was thought off.

Elfrieda drove back to the camp. It was suppertime, as she entered the first house, the group was at dinner table eating by dim candlelight, the city had turned off the lights to save electricity. It was weird to observe those silent faces in near darkness, when she said: "God has answered our prayers, we are moving tonight." The suspense was almost like in that Passover night. On to the next building she went, and to all the twelve houses the glad news came that they were to be ready by 8:00 pm.

They were all ready when the trucks came to pick them up. It went quietly and smoothly. The military blocked all traffic on the streets leading to the railway station, so that the trucks could get through fast. An ambulance was sent to the city hospital to pick up Mrs. Janzen, who was in the maternity ward and already in labor. They carried her out on a stretcher and put her on the train. The baby arrived a week later at sea!

There were 40 freight boxcars of that train waiting for the refugees, cars with no windows, only one big sliding door. The Army trucks ran into trouble when they couldn't turn around at the railroad station, one of them had a flat tire and blocked the entrance. That fiasco delayed the train by two hours.

Peter coming back by car from Bremerhaven got there just in time after he briefly checked out the empty camp. He saw Colonel Stinson on the platform who was busy, but obviously happy. The boxcars seemed loaded and filled with supplies, even stovepipes were sticking out of the partially closed boxcar doors.

In my opinion, the flat tire and the two-hour delay must have been on God's agenda, to get Peter back to Berlin in time in his car. As he entered his apartment, it looked deserted, the phone just rang, somebody who had periodically called to see if Peter had come back. Peter asked: "Where is Elfrieda?" The voice at the other end: "We are all in the train on the Berlin-Lichterfelde-West station. HURRY to get here before we leave!" Obviously *God-of-the-Splitsecond* in control here too.

Back to the railroad scene and the waiting train: The only passenger car behind the engine of the train had sick people and Elfrieda as a nurse was attending to them. Peter jumped on the train and they finally took off at about 2:00am on Friday, January 31, 1947.

PASSING THROUGH THE RED SEA

Peter and Elfriede huddled together whispering, asking what had happened since they saw each other on Tuesday. None of them could fit the things together, the why or how. Was their train ride legitimate? Where were the American soldiers? What would happen at the Russian border?

How were the 1200 people doing in the boxcars? Would anyone – or the Russian guards hear them? What if a child screemed. It was too big a problem to wrestle with, so they prayed and waited, waited and prayed. The train with the precious cargo went "stop" and "go" through the night. And at each stop on the tracks, the Dycks could hear Soviet guards talking as they walked along the train. And the Dycks worried, hoped and prayed that no sound would reveal the occupants in those 40 boxcars. If God can smite people with blindness, why not with deafness?

Finally, the train stopped and Peter jumped off to ask the engineer leaning out of the window, "Where are we?" "Helmstedt" was his brisk answer. "How far to the border?" "Two meters." In the distance he could see two Russian soldiers moving along the track inspecting trains. It would probably take an hour before they'd reach this train. Oh, no!

"Why aren't we moving?" asked Peter the engineer. That must be a stupid question, because the engineer replied: "Don't you see, the light is red?" Then suddenly the light turned green and the bar came down, and Peter scurried onto the platform as the train pulled off. In minutes they crossed the border – and the Red Sea!

Free at last! An exuberant Peter jumped off the train and opened the first boxcar behind him. "We are free – we made it!" He repeated this message from freight car to freight car and as he did, he heard those people who had been cooped up in darkness for twelve hours, sing "Nun danket alle Gott!" (the hymn: Now Thank We All Our God). As the people in the next freight car heard the song, they joined until all 40 cars were rejoicing in their deliverance. It was an awesome spontaneous praise of the redeemed like an Echo moving along the railway tracks.

*Nun danket alle Gott * Nun danket alle Gott * Nun danket alle Gott*

WHO TURNED THE LIGHT GREEN?

Just in time to avoid the inspection by the Russian soldiers? That is the obvious question and the simple answer may be "Marshall Sukolovsky of the Soviets." And yet it wasn't him either, when you know the circumstances behind it. It was really God working a miracle with perfect timing just as he used the wind to part the Red Sea for the Israelites and close it again just in time to protect them from the pursuing Egyptians.

When all those who worked hard on this Mennonite endeavor gave up hope and the ship was about to leave the harbor without the Berlin people, the heavenly agenda began to unfold.

Now as the official Washington War Records reveal, it was at one of those weekly meetings of the leaders of the four Berlin sectors (British, Russian, French and American) that General Clay of the Americans approached Russian Marshall Sukolovsky about the 1200 Mennonites from Russia and told him that he wanted to get rid off them, and about the ship waiting at Bremerhaven to take them to Paraguay. The General wanted them out of his sector.

Sukolovsky drinking some vodka with Clay agreed and Clay had papers ready for the Marshall's signature. Clay passed them over his shoulder to someone from Lt. Col. Stinton's office who dashed out of the room like a bullet. Elfrieda was notified immediately, while Peter was on the ship in Bremerhaven, and within a couple of hours the American Army moved the people from the camp to the train at Berlin-Lichterfelde.

Sukolovsky agreed reluctantly on that Friday, but sent a wire message to Moskow for permission, hoping that this permit would be refused. However, it was late in the evening, so Moskow could not respond until the next morning. And because of the speedy evacuation of those Mennonites led by Elfrieda that evening, the train passed through – **the Red Sea**.

Nobody else, but a people like the Mennonites with such abandon and faith could be the modern day example of God in action in this gigantic miracle. Their arrival in Paraguay and their courageous struggle as settlers in their colony is another heroic story of faith. I wish I could tell you how gruesome and challenging their new beginning was, but the Red Sea episode it is already the longest story in this book.

The Mennonites were told what to expect in the Chaco, part of Paraguay in South America, that hostile desert-like wasteland with no grass for animals, hardly any water and no real trees. No other settlers survived there before them, not even the native Indians. The Mennonites started with making mud bricks to build their small humble 2-room houses. They had to dig deep to find water and make a well, one for all in that village: for drinking, for those hardy oxen, and for the fields. The water was carefully doled out in dug channels. They carried that precious water on shoulder yokes like their Dutch ancestors had done. They had already learned in Berlin and in Russia to be frugal with food to sustain themselves. Now their suffering and love for each other rather than selfishness saved them. What heroes of faith who preferred this ordeal to the Gulags and persecution of the Soviet. And I can't help asking, Why did America or Canada not open their doors to them?

The above story is but a centerpiece of Peter and Elfrieda Dyck's graphic description of the Mennonite pilgrimage through World II and their new home in South America. I was graciously permitted by the authors, now in their eighties, to retell this story from their book "Up with the Rubble" (Publisher and Copyright, Herald Press, 1991).

78. Berlin Airlift and the Chocolate Pilot

What those Russian Mennonites hiding in Berlin did not know at the time was that about a year later a campaign would be initiated by the Allies in 1947 of flying food and other necessities by plane daily for an entire year. This operation was called the "Berlin Air Lift" (Luftbrücke) meaning a bridge over troubled people cut off from the rest of the country.

It happened because the Soviets tried to cut off the capital city of Berlin from the other occupied sectors, actually intending to take over the entire Eastern section of the country under Soviet Communist control. Berlin was like an island in Soviet territory and only accessible by train and by one single highway which was under Allied control. And the scheme of the Soviets was to block train and highway access. That put the Berlin population in a dangerous position in their need for food and fuel, which was not available in their bombed-out city and non-existing stores.

The Allies, meaning the Americans, the British and French, saw that as a challenge and a show of power by the Soviets. So they decided to supply the needs of the Berliners with an around-the-clock, or as we would say today "24/7" schedule of planes dropping supplies at the Berlin-Tempelhof airport.

About 800 planes did that routine daily and there was a flight every 30 seconds. This went on from June 14, 1948, to May 12, 1949 for about a year. Even Australians and Canadians helped in this effort. This was a highly organized flight schedule. If one of the planes missed the proper spot for dropping his load, he had to continue waiting in the air corridor above to try it again.

This Berlin Blockade by the Soviets was the first international crisis of the Cold War during the occupation of post-war Europe. Berliners were grateful for this lifeline from heaven and shared it with those in need in their city.

And here comes the part of the "Chocolate Pilot" as he was called by Berliner kids, or it became known as the "Flight of the Little Vittles". The Pilot, Gail Halverson, started with this idea on his own and he was afraid that his supervisor would reprimand or fire him if he'd find out. Halverson got a lot of handkerchiefs, tied each end into a knot to make a kind of parachute and filled each with gum, candy and a chocolate bar. When he was done with his flight mission, he dropped those handkerchiefs from the sky. At first people thought it was propaganda of a kind. Until they opened these tiny parachutes falling from the sky. How would they know which one of the planes has these goodies for the kids? The pilot communicated to them saying he would wiggle his wing flaps when he came to Tempelhof.

Kids waited patiently for this special plane and treated this sweet "Manna" from the air like treasures to be shared. Somehow those "enemies of ours" are not such bad people, the defeated Germans thought. It created so much goodwill. Halverson's supervisor thought it was a great idea. Some schools in the USA even adopted a plan to make these handkerchief parachutes with sweets for the good pilot.

The "Chocolate Pilot" continued his good work when flying over Bosnia and other places in later years. He even got a national award for his unique goodwill mission. His name and deed is even recorded in the National World War II records, imagine.

The Berlin Airlift was the greatest humanitarian effort in the world. There were 200,000 flights in one year, about 800 in a day, on plane flying in every 30 seconds day and night. If one of the planes missed the right spot to drop its load, the pilot had to continue flying around in the spiral waiting line, because the next pilot was already in the path. Much like planes circling about Kennedy Airport in New York today.

These planes of the Airlift transported about 2.5 million tons of food and supplies. Two-thirds of it was coal to keep Berliners warm. This program provided even more tons than they would have been able to transport via the train and highway.

There were about 92 million miles flown, which is the distance from earth to the sun. The cost for the USA alone was $225 million or 2.5 billion dollars in today's currency, not to consider the cost borne by the other allied nations for this effort.

It kept people alive with milk for the babies, food for the hungry, medicine for the sick, clothing for many, and coal and wood. Electricity was practically non-existent in those ruins.

That effort eventually humiliated the controlling Soviets and united the other Allies all the more to concentrate on the western part of Europe. It divided Germany into East and West, but the Marshall plan helped to get West Germany on its feet quickly.

Who cares? Who knows the moving story of the "Chocolate Pilot"? I wonder myself because I was admitted to the hospital on the weekend when New Orleans was hit by the great flood "Katrina" in August 2006. People were upset that food and water was not provided soon enough, as one of my nurses said to me.

"Well, why not?' I answered, "we could have flown in stuff with helicopters and dropped it to the people below. Just like we did in the Berlin Airlift with planes about 60 years ago back in 1947.

"Oh, what was that? I don't know about it. I wasn't born yet," said the nurse and I added, "Did you hear of the Chocolate Pilot?" And she must have told the other nurses my story because I ended up telling others about the airlift from my bedside many times.

79. Hansi, Orphan Girl for Hitler

I found a book about "Hansi" in an abandoned library stack and became interested in her story, which was published in 1973, some 40 years ago, while the "Iron Curtain", as Churchill named it, was still dividing East and West. That little girl with a lovely name of "Maria Anne" lived in a small village in Czechoslovakia and must have been my age, while I was being raised in Galizia nearby. Her parents were also ethnic Germans peacefully coexisting with the Czechs, until Hitler invaded her country.

Marie Anne was called "Marichen" (meaning little Mary) by her family. Her mother died in childbirth, and a good friend took the baby home and raised it as her own. Her husband disapproved and hated Marichen, they were poor peasants and had four children of their own already. Food was scarce and life was hard, so Marichen learned to put up with hardships. Her sweet, loving and caring stepmother had a deep faith in Jesus and prayed with her and taught her from the Bible. But Marichen did not know that she was not her real birthmother who loved her as her own child.

Marie Anne had a great desire to learn and she loved to read. She excelled in school and her teacher signed her up for competition with other schools, and she even became a national champion for Chzechoslovakia. Marichen was told that she had been selected to join a group of girls for training in Prague. Her mother realized the danger in this apparent honor, fearing she would never see her again, but parents had to obey these orders. Her daughter was sent to a "Westpoint for Hitler" so to speak, to be prepared for Nazi leadership, not just an opportunity to study. When the day came to leave for Prague, her mother, heartbroken and sad admonished her: "Never forget Jesus, don't forget to pray and trust Him!" not realizing, what brainwashing and subtle rewards would do to that young heart. She loved Praque, the so-called "Golden City" or "Paris of the East" with its magnificent ancient history, its grandiose buildings, palaces, towers and the many bridges over the river Moldau.

Before long, the "shackles of home" fell off to be exchanged with brassy, ostentatious garlands of a promising future, whose heir she was as a "child of the New Age." The rigid discipline and tasks made her insensitive to the quiet voice of her heart and the beckoning of her home. But she could not forget her mother, the person most dear to her. Why was she often reminded of her? She no longer could believe her mother's Bible. O yes, she still believed in a Supreme

Being, but he or it was more like Intelligence, Force, rather than that Jewish God, and Jesus? If God is so wise, how could he make such a mistake and decide to send Jesus, the Savior to the Jews, why not to a better race?

Someone gave her the nickname "Hansi", the girl who turned out to be an admired leader and model for others. Among the things to do, they wrote letters daily to unnamed soldiers in battle to encourage them. That mail called "Feldpost" did not require any stamps and was treated like airmail, arrived at the soldiers at the front even before food got there.

One of the soldiers with a very impressive handwriting and many beautifully composed pages soon found a way into her heart. She wrote to him every day and was hoping to see him someday, maybe marry him (but she was not supposed to entangle herself into such commitments too soon). They were raised to be "pure and clean for the Glorious Reich." Even romance was controlled by Hitler!

One day, a young man, named Rudy stood in the doorway of her dormitory. Hansi was just coming down the stairway, when she recognized the face of that man. In shock, she raced up the stairs and into her room. What now? Apparently, the directress of the place thought it was ok for both of them to get a couple of hours off.

The letter friendship developed into a real love. Rudy proposed to her, but she fought against her heart, she was only a peasant girl, he came from a noble and wealthy family. He won over her resistance and she accepted the ring he slipped on her finger that weekend. Rudy was such a charmer at the dinner table and the manager of the dormitory permitted Hansi to visit his family for a day. The home was as Hansi had feared, elegant, austere, and his mother could not reveal her disapproval of her son's engagement. But his sister Annemarie and Hansi became great friends.

However, trouble was brewing at home and eventually the letters of her fiancé revealed that he gave in. The engagement was off. A humiliated and broken young maiden sent her ring to his parents. And you can imagine the rest.

What I found interesting in this book was not just this scene of an unhappy relationship. But the whole journey of this young girl so subtly mislead and yet so blindly dedicated to the demands of the Great Reich and its Führer that she willingly sacrificed everything for him. No more thoughts about marriage for her either. But she could not make herself see the desperate situation her country was in. Blind belief in the Führer, even as the bombs were dropping on Prague and the ruins and burning buildings collapsing around her.

One day she was sent to report to a refugee children's home and was given the order to take about thirty children to some country destination which would be safer there than the city of Praque. For the first time she realized what responsibility it was, but when there wasn't enough room in the train for the children, she threatened the station manager to clear the compartments of the other passengers – pronto. Hansi returned to the city, but did not stay long, it was in danger of being captured by Russians. She managed to leave on the last train before the enemy arrived.

It wasn't long before she and other women were taken to a labor camp of a Czech estate. They were treated roughly, not even given anything to drink or eat at times, but were beaten when they broke down in exhaustion on the fields. Hansi couldn't believe this harsh reality. What happened? Worse, the manager of the farm delighted in letting the Russian soldiers know that there were women out here available. Why not invite them in? There was nowhere they could escape to, the gates were locked at night and the fences too high for escape.

They called themselves "slave women". Night after night those Russian solders arrived for their prey. Hansi was spared somehow but she thought, "If any one of those brutes would ever touch me, I'll fight like a wildcat." Somehow she discovered a hiding place for the women in a distant hey barn which had a small obscure door in the back of the barn. When it was dark, they would sneak into the barn to sleep and before the sun rose, they'd tiptoe back to their designated sleeping quarters.

One night Hansi was going to lead her friends to that hideout again, but as she reached to open the squeaky door, something warned her not to go inside. "Why not?" the girls protested. Again, she stepped forward and she felt the same strong warning, "don't go in there tonight." The girls were puzzled. It turned out that someone had betrayed them. That night the Russians entered the barn and could not find the women, so they poked at the heystack with their bayonets in anger, but no one was there. The next day at the end the work in the field, after the manager had left them (he didn't expect them to run away) Hansi said to the girls, " I don't know about you, but I am going to run away tonight I must get out of here before it's too late."

Knowing how risky it was and that the country was searched for escapees, she thought that the others would stay, but they all went along with her through the wooded areas and deserted fields. These women were marked people, having to wear a white armband. If they didn't, they could be shot on sight. Eventually the girls took off on their own one by one. Only two of them were left, Hansi and another girl, named Micherle.

They continued inspite of the rain, often drenched to the bone and being hungry. People in the towns kept their doors locked and ignored these refugees, too many of them asking for food and shelter. One night, exhausted and soaking wet, they knocked at a "Gasthaus" (restaurant). An old man opened the door carefully and looked at them pitifully. "May we just come in and warm ourselves a bit?" He hesitantly let them in and offered them to sit down by the fire, while he went out to bring some warm soup – what a delight!

Then Hansi asked if he knew where they could cross the border through the "Niemandsland" (no man's land) to get to the West. They must have touched his heart – he confided and told them that there was a ferry man by the river who could show them the way for some pay. They were heading for the door, but he offered them a bed upstairs. The next morning, both girls walked to the river and found that ferry man with his boat. Halfway across, Hansi told him that she didn't want to ferry across but rather wanted to find out the secret passage to the West and she opened her secret compartment in her rucksack and showed him some jewels, money, and a silk scarf. He took it and told them to come in the evening at dusk and hide in the trees until a guide would arrive to bring them across.

When Hansi got to the designated spot, more people were hesitantly arriving, even families with little children's whose mouth was tied with a scarf so they would really be quiet. These refugees were nervously huddling in the hideout grass when it began to rain. They too were waiting for that ferry guide. Then at a silent signal, they started to crawl through the high grass and along shrubs up to the barren hill. What if the Russians could see them and start shooting? They heard shots nearby and hid frightened in the grass.

All the sudden, a child cried nearby. "Oh, no, they will now see us!" Hansi crawled over to find a little, perhaps 3-year old girl calling for Mommy. "Hush little bunny, we will help you find Mommy if you are quiet, but you mustn't cry!" While she was comforting the child, she was wondering why she took on another burden – surely, now they will be discovered and shot. So Hansi and her pal Micherle took the little girl by the hand and practically dragged her uphill in the rain. And the girl did not make a sound – as if she sensed the danger they were in.

Over beyond the hill were the American soldiers if they could make it to them. The little girl was exhausted, so Hansi took her on her shoulder and she fell asleep. The two women made it and they could see a house which looked like an Army station. They knocked at the door and a smiling American GI stood in the doorway. "Can you please help this little girl? Her lips are blue, she might die from pneumonia." She said this in German, because she didn't speak English, but the soldier must have understood their predicament and welcomed them to come in. Other soldiers came and brought some sweaters and warm clothes to wear. Again, they tried to communicate in sign language that this was a child who lost its mother. Maybe she was shot on the hill? "Can we leave this girl with you, perhaps the Blue Cross can help find the mother?" A cook in a white outfit came in to bring some warm food. This was too good to be true. What would be the payoff? As they were heading to the door, they heard, "Please stay for the night, we good men." They were scared, but they were too tired to leave.

The amazing part of this story is that it may well have been that their compassion for the lost little girl and the risk they took to drag her along may have saved their lives. Because Russians adore children, and seeing these two women holding the little one between them may have softened their hearts this time. Perhaps *"God-of-the-Splitsecond"* graciously protecting them?

The next morning they handed the little girl to the Red Cross station in case they found the mother of this little orphan. I will omit whole sections of this dramatic story of "Hansi", but point out, that her frequent reminder of mother and envisioning her in her evening devotions reading, praying or singing some hymn, was because her mother was truly praying for her daughter ever since she left home. It may well be her prayers that undergirded this dramatic escape to the American west zone – and to freedom.

In their ongoing journey, the two women stopped in a pharmacy to buy some snacks. A young lady was talking to the pharmacist turned around to see who that familiar voice was. Guess, who that lady was, Rudy's sister Annemarie. A coincidence? Their family had to leave their grand estate and managed to get to this particular village (out of all places in Germany). An awkward embrace for Hansi but a happy reunion for Rudy's sister. It is a touching story of reconciliation and new hope, eventually breaking through the dark clouds of despair.

Most of all, Hansi eventually found her dear mother who had been praying for her daughter without knowing what nightmare and depression she was going through in the turmoil when her world was coming apart. Eventually even Rudy, the soldier missing in the war, returned. And there was indeed a happy ending to this story, even a new beginning in America for both of them and for their children. But that nightly hiding place at camp and that dangerous run over the hill to freedom, were the greatest *God-of-the-Splitsecond* moments in her life.

(Excerpt from the book, entitled "Hansi, the Girl who loved the Swastika", Tyndale House Publishers, 1973).

80. Corrie ten Boom at the Prison Gate

I believe, there is hardly anyone who has not heard about Corrie ten Boom or seen that moving film "The Hiding Place" about her life and suffering in the concentration camp during the Nazi regime. I am sure, you were as amazed at the fortitude and inner strength which she and other prisoners showed in the midst of inhuman, cruel torture and persecution. And you were probably as amazed at her grace and love inspite of all her suffering, that she devoted the rest of her life to spreading the Good News of Jesus in her travels around the world.

Instead of retiring in a comfortable home, Corrie became a "Tramp for the Lord" as she called herself. Her entire life story is a testimony to the strength and endurance of saints in the fire of affliction. The "Watchmaker's Daughter" became an ambassador of love, even in the impossible moment she found herself one day when a man approached her after a church service where she spoke.

He was one of those cruel guards and he came to ask her for forgiveness. Hatred welled up in her heart for what he and others had done to millions of innocent people. She remembered how those perpetrators tried to destroy her own people, the Dutch, by starving many to death and mistreating them as captives. "No, I can't forgive him," she fought, but the Holy Spirit tenderly tugged at her heart.

"Alright, if you help me to do it, I will." No, it wasn't cheap grace and forgiveness. Someone had paid a great price for it. Corrie and her older sister Betsy still found some good things to be thankful for in that concentration camp. And you know, why they were sent there because the ten Boom family were one of those who helped Jews find a shelter and hideout from the Nazis. They even built a camouflaged entrance to the upper room of her house and these refugees had to be very quiet and not come out in the daytime.

It reminds me of the "underground railroad" in America which sympathetic people established for the slaves to work their way to freedom. Well, apparently somebody betrayed the ten Boom family and as a result, all of them including their aging parents were sent to concentration camp.

I suggest you read the many books which Corrie wrote, such as "The Watchmaker's Daughter", "The Hiding Place" and others. Her whole life was a miracle of grace and towards her final years she worshipped as a member of Chuck Swindoll's church in California. I would have loved to have met her.

These two sisters kept their spirits up in gratefulness and trust in their Lord. They always found something to be thankful for, even for the lice in their beds. Their barrack was so infested with those pesty creatures that it kept the women-guards away from it. The women prisoners were left alone most of the time and they could talk freely and pray and study the Bible. That simple Bible which Corrie and Betsy were able to hide in their clothes or some secret place. It was a miracle that the guards did not find it or take it away during the entire prison time! When they had to undress in the main hallway for a shower, Betsy and Corrie managed to hide it underneath the bench somewhere. Or when they were body-searched, they just prayed that the guard would not detect it. It apparently worked.

Another reason Corrie was thankful to the Lord was for the tasks given to them. When her older sister Betsy could barely dig the heavy soil and nearly collapsed, they changed her work assignment. Betsy and Corrie told the guard that they could knit very fast, promptly they were ordered to join the knitters of socks which eventually went to the soldiers or elsewhere. Well, the knitting circle became a bible study group. Other women, sick and desperate wanted to hear more of the wonderful news of the Gospel while they were busy knitting at the table.

But let me share with you one of the many stories that impressed me. The one I want to pen down here is definitely a *God-of-the-Splitsecond* event, namely the daily routine roll call, for which the women in the camp were awakened in the middle of the night by a shrill sergeant whistle to line up for roll call. They hardly had anything to wear, but they had to stand in line outside in the bitter cold, even in the winter to wait for their number instead of their name to be called and they had to answer "here".

Usually, the women were directed to do as follows, when their number was up, they had to join a group either on the right or on the left. They never knew where either group would end up, either the workplace or the gas chamber. Towards the end of the war, some of the prisoners were released from the camp. They were sent to a shower room to be cleaned up and given some clothes to wear, so they would look representable to the public.

On one of those brisk mornings, Corrie's number was called and she thought, "That's it. Now I must go to the gas chamber." But instead she was asked to join a group which would eventually be released. Corrie writes in her books, that her release was actually a mistake by the guard, but that the Lord turned that one around. He still had plenty of work for her to do outside the camp.

She and another woman, after being given a bath and some clean clothes to put on, were shoved beyond the prison gate. Corrie said, the first thing she noticed was color, the color green, flowers, sunshine, and it was blinding to one who only saw grey and dirt in the camp. They noticed the kind of clothes other people were wearing. The two women got on a train going to Northern Holland, however, they learned that it was still occupied by the Nazis.

As they left the train station in Holland, they were given directions where the hospital clinic was. Tired, exhausted, looking like ghosts in clothes, they found themselves in a waiting room and a friendly nurse in a bright white uniform asking: "What can we do for you? What would you like?" Corrie couldn't think of anything she wanted more than a bath, a bathroom with warm water running in a tub and her soaking in it and using clean towels. Have you ever craved a bath like that? You would be, if you hadn't seen one for over a year.

Their sagging spirits were uplifted with a delicious soup and a tray of tasty food to nourish them and that gorgeous bath with bubbles was like heaven to Corrie! It was so nice to be cared for by loving people, by their cheerfulness and love. And it was lovely to be again in a world of "color" and green grass, trees and flowers and most of all, to be free.

Another *God-of-the-Splitsecond* moment. The nurse asked where her original home was, "I am from denHaag," Corrie answered, "Well, I am from denHaag too and I remember a lovely teacher I had, her name was Corrie." She probably did not recognize her in that poor starved condition. But wasn't it wonderful and a sign of encouragement to Corrie, to have that same nurse there who had once been her pupil? Out of thousands of nurses in Holland?

(This story paraphrased from the book, entitled "The Watchmaker's Daughter" by Jean Watson, published by Fleming H. Revell Company, 1982)

81. Freedom Dance – Bolshoi Ballet

The headlines "Russian Dancers Defect" created a stir in the Los Angeles area as well as the rest of the free world. On September 16, 1979, a Russian couple, the lead dancers performing as Romeo and Juliet escaped after the final curtain call into the dark, while KGB officers frantically raced after the van that had picked them up.

The getaway is still all the more amazing, considering that it was not pulled off by professionals, or by the CIA or FBI, but by some fumbling amateurs, ordinary people who didn't even look for such an assignment which was amazing. How did this simple home-loving couple, the young woman Sasha and her withdrawn husband George, the vegetable-selling truck driver, get involved in this drama?

It apparently started with a downtown shopping spree of Sasha at the Broadway Mall in Los Angeles. Her husband George dropped her off nearby because she wanted to browse and just look, taking their 5-year old daughter Kim along for a stroll. Her dad gave her some change for an ice-cream. They promised to be waiting for him at the same spot at 3:00 pm when he expected to be finished with his vegetable sale from his flatbed truck.

Sasha and Kim enjoyed the Mall and the many interesting things and the people they saw. Kim munched on her ice-cream and noticed the window display of a pet shop, parrots, hamsters and rabbits in their cages. She couldn't wait to go inside, but she had to finish her ice-cream cone first. Then it was Sasha's turn to browse in the big glamorous department store. In the women's section she looked at bathing suites, blouses and sports clothes. As she was browsing through a rack of designer jeans, she heard voices, a man and a woman talking softly in Russian, a language one seldom hears in Los Angeles. Her parents who escaped from Russia many years ago still spoke Russian to one another, but Sasha was brought up American.

Surprised, Sasha turned around and saw a young couple, an athletic man and a younger beautiful blonde who was trying on a sweater, which her companion admired. But Sasha noticed another man standing nearby, a tall heavy-built man with a stern look watching every move of the couple. He must be their taxi driver, she thought. She took her daughter Kim by the hand and moved on to browse elsewhere.

Sasha picked a beautiful dress that she liked and took it into the cubicle to try it on. Of course, she couldn't afford to buy it but can't one have dreams? Her hands gliding over the soft fabric, she felt like a princess, almost forgot her daughter Kim who waited for her sitting in a chair outside. As Sasha headed for the mirror in the hallroom, she ran into the young lady from Russia again, who apologized in Russian for being in her way. And Sasha answered in Russian, and that's when that innocent unsuspecting chance meeting occurred, where Sasha Rolling and Valentina Koslovo chatted, while her husband Leonid paced the floor outside, with that tight-lipped man standing in the shadow watching both of them. Sasha thought they were tourists, but learned that they were ballet dancers with the Bolshoi Ballet. Again, the stern eyes of that man met Sasha's and she hurried away with Kim. She did not know as most people were unaware that the Bolshoi Ballet troupe stationed for their performance in Los Angeles was packed with KGB bodyguards, 42 of them for the 125 dancers, one for every three to watch over every move onstage and off.

At the agreed-upon street corner, George picked up his wife and daughter, but it had been raining and his sale was washed out too. Not many customers cared to come out in the rain, so he had a truckload full of vegetables left over. He decided to swing by a Christian mission station where he donated the load to their kitchen, rather than having the vegetables rot on his truck.

Sasha told him about the couple she met in the Mall. Soon after they came home, the telephone rang which she answered. A man at the other end of the line spoke with a heavy Russian accent and Sasha occasionally said "da da" during the conversation. George tried to read the impressions on his wife's serious face. Then she held her hand over the phone and said to him: "Remember the dancers I met today? He is asking if we can help them. The man and his wife want to stay in the United States." But before the man at the other end of the phone could say more, he whispered, "Someone is coming, I'll call you later." And he hung up the phone.

Puzzled and perplexed, both of them pondered the meaning of this strange phone call. Was this a crank call, what can THEY do? But they waited for two hours and no calls. Did these people get into trouble? Should they ask someone else? So they prayed and asked God to help in this problem and guide them. "I know what we need to do, we need to ask for legal advice." said George. "But whom, we can't afford a lawyer," replied Sasha.

The rest of the story I can only present in brief sketches because of the lack of space.

A phone call to George's brother-in-law, Steve Tilden, a detective and the ramifications led to a rescue plan by him and his buddy into which the inexperienced and frightened couple were drawn into. The event was definitely unscripted, although the KGB guards of the ballet group were leaked a hint of an anticipated escape, assuming the FBI was behind it.

Tilden phoned his pal, Kirk Harper, and they both drove over to George's house to find out more about the matter even though it was late Friday night. They asked, "Do you know who called, has the caller left a number or what?" While they were waiting and talking, the phone rang late that night. Sasha picked up the phone, it was the same voice on the other end. The man asked if they could pick them up the next morning at 11:00 am at the next street corner from the University Hilton Hotel where the Bolshoi Ballet troupe stayed. They would be coming out of the hotel and start jogging along Figuera Street.

The brother-in-law and his buddy were eager to go along with this odd situation, while the couple was scared stiff. Anyway, they decided to take George into their van the next morning and drive to the hotel. They parked nearby so that they could watch the couple coming out of the hotel. George and Tilden were hovering in the back, taking turns to watch the entrance of the hotel with a binocular. Promptly at 10:00 am a couple in jogging suits hurried out of the revolving door and ran along the mentioned road.

"Ok, they are coming!" yelled Tilden to Kirk at the wheel, "get ready to drive slowly when I tell you, and we'll grab them and pull'em into the van." As they were about to pass the van, the two "kidnapped" the startled couple. And they spoke perfect English with no foreign accent. Soon clues indicated that they had caught the wrong couple, these were not the Bolshoi couple but American tourists. What now? Will the KGB or FBI have noticed this or will they be reported? The man offered his wallet, but Tilden opened the van door and let them out: "No thanks. It's ok, it was a mistake. Have a good day!"

The two police-detectives didn't know that the ballet couple was detained from leaving the hotel for their daily jogging round because an informer leaked a secret to the chief KGB Major Markoff that someone from the group plans to defect. So he gave house arrest orders to all dancers – no one was to leave the hotel building until their departure on Monday, no usual shopping sprees or whatever. Security was increased, every one was being watched by his or her body guard. And Leonid received a personal warning from the Major. That made him and Valentina cautious and wonder if they would be able to make their leap to freedom.

When the three men arrived at home, they were too embarrassed to tell Sasha about the botched up kidnapping. The kitchen had an inviting smell because Sasha was ready to serve them some delicious soup. She told these hungry guys, that shortly after they left for the hotel, a call came from the same man, saying that the couple was unable to come out at 11:00 am, but that they wanted to defect after the last curtain call of the Sunday performance. Could we have a car ready for them then? As a confirmation that George and Sasha would go through with the rescue, "the man would leave two tickets at the box office reserved for Mr. and Mrs. George Rollins. If the tickets were picked up, the contact would know that the plan was set and that a car would be waiting for them behind the auditorium after the final curtain." He would make himself known to Sasha by asking: "How is the weather in Moskau?" and she was to tell him what kind of car would be waiting outside.

Harper and Tilden wondered about it and asked, "but where will the defectors be?" "On stage," replied Sasha, "and they expect a big applause for the final curtain call." There was a fire escape door on the east side of the stage.

Someone would have to disarm the alarm on this exit. Harper and Tilden wondered, how they could get in there to disarm the door alarm. "There's the KGB, the FBI, and the LAPD Intelligence. We can't just walk in there, we'd be fired." George suggested that maybe they'd better call the FBI. But the two felt there was not enough time, it would be delayed in bureaucracy. It was already late Saturday afternoon. So the two decided to arrive at the auditorium in an official car as Fire Department Inspectors wearing badges and carrying a clipboard on their way to inspect the building. They walked up the steps and waved to security guards nearby, but an FBI man stopped them inside. Tilden reached into his pocket, pulled out a badge and said confidentially: "Special Event and Safety Protection."

The FBI man stepped to the side to enquire via his lapel microphone. No, they didn't have their names on the roster. But Tilden insisted, "We are here for the quarterly Egress and Equipment Inspection," Harper added, "I personally sent the teletype notification to the FBI," and added, "Now if you want us to go ahead and close this building to public access, you got it." Soon they were permitted to pass through into the auditorium. While some FBI guy watched them, the two busied themselves checking out wiring, locks, fire signals, and the exit doors. After awhile, the FBI man walked out, thinking these two knew what they were doing. Yup, that was the quiet moment they needed to do the job without leaving tell-tale signs. And they drove to their home again.

Sunday morning George and Sasha went to their church as usual. He was not listening much to the sermon but was preoccupied with the ballet group. What have they gotten themselves into? Why should they be the ones to help them? Why put themselves into such danger. No, he mustn't let Sasha get involved. There must be another way – not them. Suddenly his attention was drawn to the sermon which was almost over. What did the pastor say? Oh, it's the story of the Good Samaritan and the other guys, the Levite, the Priest who passed by with a good excuse. "It's not MY business". But somehow he felt as if the Savior pleaded with him, "if there is the dying man lying, will you pass over too?" "Do it for me. Help them."

And his mind turned to the two people wanting freedom more than anything. In agony over this parable tugging at his heart and the begging of those Russian strangers seemed to melt into one picture. "Alright, Lord, if you want us to help these, you must give us wisdom and help us." Daughter Kim went to stay with grandmother neither of them knew about this. In the afternoon Sasha prepared to go to the ballet performance at the famous Shriner Auditorium. She found her green taffeta prom dress, the only formal gown she owned which still fit her. There was the beige lace tablecloth, an heirloom from her Russian grandmother, and she draped it over her shoulders. Her hair was all done up.

George was amazed how beautiful she looked and gave her a kiss, as she stepped up into his vegetable truck to take off for the ballet. What a strange combination, a fine lady in an old beatup truck going to a ballet! Sasha tried to find a parking spot and drove around the block three times. She finally turned into a parking lot across the street and the attendant looked surprised, "You want to park here? It's 10 dollars." Sasha was fumbling to find enough money, while the gala crowd in rich-looking cars behind her honked impatiently. The man finally let her park anyway to move the traffic.

Sasha was very nervous and apparently didn't ask for the right name at the box office. "No, there are no tickets!" the person replied. Was it a letdown? Finally, after stating different names, she thought of "Mr. and Mrs. George Rollins," and she was handed two tickets.

The ballet was a new experience for her and she was fascinated. During intermission, she remained in her seat waiting for the agreed upon person to arrive. She was so nervous and felt her heart beating wildly – frightened of the whole thing and praying for George, that the Lord would help them through this. As the light started flickering, somebody sat down in an empty seat behind her and tapped her on her shoulder and whispered, "Don't look behind you," and he said the clue sentence: "What time is it in Moskau?" Sasha replied: "It's a white van" and after awhile the man got out of the seat and left the auditorium.

The KGB drama developing behind the scene was another matter of which the "four helpers" had no idea, starting with the leak of a "mole" to chief KGB Major Markoff and the subsequent house arrest for the troupe. They traced that phone call and learned that the lead dancers were the ones to defect. Also they traced the identity of the home of Sasha and George.

During the last act of the ballet, a burly man walked up the main isle and his eyes met Sasha's, who quickly looked away, hoping not to be recognized because she realized the same stern face that had watched the ballerina in the department store. As she looked up, he was still staring at her and then he walked out quickly to find Markoff backstage and tell him, who the defectors are – the Koslovs. In seconds, they had the five leading KGB guards backstage ready to intervene in the plot.

It seemed like the final curtain call wouldn't end, five times the crowd clapped and cheered. But like a miracle, inspite of the "guards" ready to snap Valentina and Leonid, they were able to race to the fire door and jump into the waiting van and dash off in a hurry. The five KGB piled into a rented car and chased after them. But Harper and Tilden blocked the driveway with their VW and drove ahead of them to distract and mislead the angry KGB guards.

It is amazing how the blundering and frightening act of those novices and the help of two friends accomplished the escape – right to the home of the couple where they changed into some civilian clothes. Nobody found them. (Today they could search the Internet). Next morning, Tilden and Harper drove the two Russians to the police to report on the defection and seek their help for the next step. The police couldn't believe that all this happened without the FBI, the police or whoever. The KGB with the help of a translator tried to persuade the Koslovs to return with them to Moskau. It was all a bad dream and manipulation they told them, but the two insisted that it was their own choice to stay in the USA.

The ballet dancers eventually continued in their career in another city. The interesting thing I gleaned from this book "Freedom Dance" was the apparent coincidence of Valentina meeting another woman of Russian descent and the other factors woven into the story of escape. Their faith in the Lord, tell of His guidance and watching over us. Again *God-of-the-Splitsecond* in a strange and scary drama.

(This story is paraphrased from the book, entitled "Freedom Dance" by Dallas L. Barnes, published by Here's Life Publishers, Inc. San Bernadino, 1985. Later assigned to Tyndale House Publishers)

82. Livingstone and Africa

The fascinating story of a man whose life work has become synonymous with Africa, a vast continent which had been a dark mysterious land before. The great, dedicated explorer and physician, David Livingstone, made a difference. I am including this unusual man in my stories, because there is one event in his life that impressed me greatly. It fits into my GDS-collection in this book. But wait, let me tell you other things about him first.

David Livingstone was born in Scotland in 1813 and he lived till 1873. His father forbade him to read any religious books because he didn't want him to become a preacher, I guess. But he loved to read and to learn about life, so he read anything on science and travel he could get his hands on. When he was 10 years old he was sent to work, not because his parents were mean, but because the family needed his meager wage to be able to eat. David missed out on his "teenage years". Do you know that teens or tweens are an American invention and a recent one? This young boy was working in the local cotton factory for 14 long hours a day. So there was no time to study or go to school. He was more interested in educating himself than his work at the loom. Imagine, he even had a book propped up at his spinning-jenny so he could snatch a sentence in those one-minute pauses of the machine, and think about that thought while he worked.

Imagine our long coffee breaks or other times we waste so easy lately on the cell phone texting or checking emails? And the ongoing noise of pop music in the stores and malls that snatch our own thoughts, so that our minds are bombarded with the singer's story. Could we try and do what the determined boy did while he worked? I mean, could we slip in some good idea instead of being distracted with trivia and noise? Meanwhile that 10-year old worker learned about travels and the world, natural history, and science. The other factory workers thought he was odd and unfriendly, while he learned about Marco Polo and read Wilberforce's work on slavery in those precious free minutes.

At the age of 23, he was able to enter Glasgow University in Scotland and lateron Oxford, and he studied medicine and Greek and theology. Eventually he became pastor but he was too shy for the task, so he entered missionary work and was sent to what they called then the "Dark Continent" of Africa. On that long voyage by ship, the captain taught him how to take astronomical observations, how to read the stars in the sky and tell where they were on the ocean. That skill became very important to him later in the interior of Africa, when he was plodding his path through deserts and jungles with his expeditions. There were no road maps then, in fact, no white man had ever walked there before. Livingstone walked about 250,000 miles through the dangerous interior. What a man! God had another job for Livingstone waiting for him and his father worried needlessly, one that only a man with his stamina, determination and self-sacrifice could accomplish. So when you hear "Africa", you can say "Livingstone".

Again, reading stars and constellations proved a vital skill for him later on his many explorations through the interior. He acquired the skill to make accurate records of his observations in geology, botany and natural history. His journals of his travels are a treasure of discovery.

In 1844 he married Mary Moffat, the daughter of a missionary doctor in Africa who founded the mission station in Kurman. She was just the right helpmate for him and put up with many dangers and hardships that another person couldn't have. Mary and their children even tracked along on those expeditions, or struggled on the muddy rivers in their canoes along with their African helpers. They were in danger from snakes, poison plants, wild animals, all of it, and why?

Livingstone wasn't just on an ego trip. He wanted to help the African people with his medical care, he taught them how to dig wells, how to get more planting out of the meager soil, how to make things and improve their lives. But he wasn't just a "do-good" European, who'd boss those people around. His heart was filled with the love of Jesus and his trust in the Lord God of the Universe. He spoke their language and tribes and chiefs considered him their friend.

His great dream was the unknown land to the North. If he could find a passage to the interior and a river that could be used to open up the isolated interior for travel and commerce, it could help the African people. Livingstone was unlike those Portuguese and other exploiters who invaded unsuspecting natives and snatched them into slavery. He was

trying to find Lake Ngami, but he had to cross the inhos-
pitable Kalahari Desert, he was the first European to do
that. He also discovered the river Zouga, a majestic stream.
Another discovery was the great river Zambezi. His careful
journals, maps, and nature studies were valuable, as was
his knowledge of the dangerous tsetse fly that caused the
dreaded fever. Eventually he sent his wife and his four children back to England, it was too dangerous for them to go
along with him.

Meanwhile, his fame reached England and Oxford
University as well as the Queen, who gave him a distin-
guished honor. They wanted him to stay in England, but he
refused and went back to Africa, still driven by his objective
to find that waterway. He traveled with only a few supplies
enough to survive, and just the nautical almanac, logarithm
tables and his Bible. Unhealthy fever racked him all the time,
he encountered hostile chiefs and the journey became almost
impossible, sometimes the natives turned away or refused to
go on. Then the chief and the tribe of Makolo welcomed him
and gave him helpers for his next trip.

Livingstone eventually discovered the great magnificent
Victoria Falls. He also sailed in a little boat about 2,500 miles
to Bombay, India to reenter Africa from another side to find
the source of the Nile River. He discovered Lake Tanganyika
as well, a lake of fresh water about 12,000 square miles,
bigger than Belgium. He became seriously ill with fever,
because a porter deserted Livingstone and took his medicine
chest with him.

Somehow a reporter by the name of H.M. Stanley of
the New York Herald found the ailing explorer and wanted
to take this famous man back to America but Livingstone
wouldn't leave his beloved Africa, his heart was in Africa.
On his last journey he could no longer sit up but had to be
carried by his helpers on a flat tray. I read about this amazing

man in an old book by an unknown author, entitled "One Hundred Great Lives" (Oldhams Press Ltd).

But now I want to share with you the story about Livingstone, which I heard many times since childhood. However, I can't find it in any books on the legendary man. Maybe the publishers took it out, supposing it to be a myth? It would be another *God-of-the-Splitsecond* moment. The story goes like this: One night, as Livingstone was sleeping in his hut in the interior of Africa, a group of warriors from a hostile tribe came to kill him. As the warriors with their spears were quietly approaching the hut, they noticed men in white gowns standing shoulder to shoulder around the house. The warriors did not expect this unusual guard and fearfully withdrew to return to their village.

When word finally reached his helpers, asking, "Who were those white warriors surrounding your hut last night?" Livingstone replied, "what warriors?" He hadn't ordered any such guards. Could it be that the Lord sent divine messengers or angels to protect him? People who have been in danger in many ways testify to the fact that someone looking like a man or woman came to their aid – and then suddenly disappeared? Think about it.

The end of that humble great man, who devoted his life to Africa is just as moving. One morning, one of his servants found Livingstone kneeling by his bedside praying, as he used to do regularly. The servant didn't want to disturb him. He came back after awhile, but noticed he didn't move. Livingstone had died in that familiar posture, being called home by his Heavenly Lord. His servants respected their beloved master and prepared for his funeral. They cut his heart out and buried it under a tree. They dried his body as best they could in the sun. Then they carried his embalmed body 1,100 miles to the coast of Zanzibar! Together with his papers, journals and instruments, they placed it on a ship back to England. Livingstone was buried in a tomb inside the Westminster Abbey in London, but his heart stayed in Africa, where could it more fittingly rest?

83. Shepherd Boy at the Cave

The fascinating story of a boy and his work, not like the one you just read about, young David working at a spinning factory in Scotland. This boy lived in the sunny parched hills of the desert in Syria near the famous Dead Sea. I have always wondered why they call it "Dead Sea". It's not because of dead fish, but because it takes water in from the River Jordan and keeps it all. No outlet, it's a dead end.

You heard about that if you try to swim in the Dead Sea, you would float on top of the water and not drown. Imagine that, a non-swimmers lake! On the shallow parts of the lake, where the water dries out, it has huge piles of white stuff – not snow, but solid chunks of salt. The Dead Sea is also a salt mine and people make money from selling salt.

Well, in those hills nearby, people send their kids to watch the goats while they graze in that area. Our shepherd boy had plenty of time on his hands. I wonder, what you would do with no books, no television, no toys. This little boy did not have the desire or opportunity to read or study, I suppose. He didn't turn out to be a doctor or explorer like David Livingstone. Nevertheless, he must have studied the landscape around him and the rocks and plants while he looked after the goats. And he had no radio or cell phone either.

So he was conscious of every sound, the chirping and buzzing of insects, and he looked out for dangerous snakes or lizards. You get the picture. Another thing he could pass the time away with, was throwing stones as far as possible. Whenever he approached a cave, he would throw in a few for fun. Maybe he was bored or wanted to check out if there were dangerous residents inside?

On one of those hot days, the shepherd boy threw some stones into one of the caves nearby. He was surprised when he heard a different sound echo from inside, his rock must have hit something hollow. He bent down to look into the dark cave and didn't know what he would find there, perhaps a dangerous animal. Curiosity killed the cat! Not this one – deep in the interior stood a few large dusty clay pots and he must have hit one. Did you know that such caves were places, where people hid valuable things from thieves or pirates?

The shepherd probably didn't know about this, but when he carefully pulled out one of this large pots or urns as they are called, he found some rolled up parchments inside with writings on them. He herded his goats to his village as soon as their grazing time was over and ran home as fast as he could. Soon word got around about those parchments, and experts and archeologists carefully examined these – they were authentic stuff. The scrolls were kept in Jerusalem, if I remember correctly. The year was 1947 and the world calls this event "The Dead Sea Scrolls."

Hardly any one knows the name of this little boy, but that shepherd became world famous for what he found in the caves. Those dusty scrolls had been carefully preserved all this time and they were handwritten by scribes who didn't just scribble things down carelessly. In that desert area were a group of monks or hermits called the Essens, who lived about 400 years before Christ. They devoted their lives to copying Holy Scripture, i.e. the Old Testament for the Jews to be read in the synagogues. (The Torah)

What is so remarkable that the Holy Scriptures were copied by scribes in the most careful way, and they were checked word for word, letter for letter four times by other scribes to make sure the previous scribe did not overlook anything. It was that sacred and important a document – the Word of God. It is only a few decades ago that we Christians started being liberal with our translations. How many versions do we have of it? Think about how carefully the King's James version was translated by a group of scholars.

Those scrolls found in the Dead Sea cave were authentic manuscripts from the book of Isaiah and other books of the Bible, but they were much older, thousands of years older than any manuscripts we had until then. In fact, they discovered a manuscript of Isaiah which was 600 years older than the one we had until the findings of the Dead Sea Scrolls. And as scholars and theologians studied the texts and compared it with newer versions of originals, they found that the words were essentially the same.

What does the shepherd boy's finding have to do with me or with you? A great deal, because it confirms to us that the Word of God, our Bible is a reliable history book and a trusted message from God for our ages and those to come. Why were they hidden in that cave for millennia and not discovered until 1947? Maybe it is another one of those *God-of-the-Splitsecond* timings for this 20th century marked by unbelief and violence, one where Nietsche's words "God is dead" echoed in rebellious as well as in desperate hearts. Nietsche is dead but God is very much alive.

84. Newton and the Ship gone Astray

While reading a biography on John Newton by Catherine Swift, I found at least one *"God-of-the-Splitsecond"* event in the tumultuous life of that old converted sea captain. The author paints a dramatic picture of the sinful debauchery of that British sailor, who eventually turned to the Lord and gave his heart to Jesus, when everyone had given up on him.

John Newton left us a legacy of hymns, one of which is the well-known "Amazing Grace," which became the motto of his changed life. Another hymn written by Newton is "How Sweet the Name of Jesus Sounds" and also the hymn "Glorious Things of Thee Are Spoken," to the tune of one of Haendel's compositions. Ironically, Hitler used the same tune for his anthem "Deutschland, Deutschland über alles", why, I don't know. Maybe because he hated the Christian text as an atheist and wanted to overrule it. I only remember the jolt I felt, when I was visiting a Canadian church back in the 50s and the congregation began to sing "Glorious Things of Thee are Spoken." I simply couldn't sing it, that tune reminded me of the horrible Nazi period, my childhood in Germany. So you kids, teens, who say you don't listen to the words, only the music. Nonsense, you listen to all of it.

After this sweeping introduction, let me share with you some episodes of Newton's eventful life that displays another "GDS-moment". John Newton was born in London in 1725 as a son of a Sea Captain. His father was very strict and ran his home more like his ship, treating his son John more like a ship's cabin boy than his own son. He was only permitted to speak when spoken too and could only sit when given permission. His mother Elizabeth was a rather affectionate person who cared deeply about their children. Their home was in the new area of London which had been rebuilt after the Great Fire of 1666. It also had many exciting souvenirs, rugs and ornaments which his captain father had brought back from his voyages around the world.

To get another picture of life in London, the splendor of a great city with the magnificent Westminster Abbey, St. Paul's Cathedral and the Royal Palace as well as Oxford and Cambridge University, and a splendid harbor. That was the home of John Newton. On Sunday mornings the Captain took John to church, the Church of England also known as the Anglican Church. The little boy had to endure long and boring rituals and chants as he recalled. But when his mother Elizabeth took him to her chapel services of a Dissenter group, he seemed to enjoy the happy, joyful gospel songs and the devotion of the believers. The old grey-haired composer Isaac Watts was there and John learned many of his songs, like "O God, Our Help in Ages Past" and many others.

John was so taken up with these services and told his mother that he wanted to become a minister some day. Yet his mother suspected that that wouldn't happen, but that John would follow in his father's footsteps and become a captain of a ship some day. Even as a little lad, he trotted behind his Captain dad to the docks. He learned a lot about ships by observing the sailors and studying the stuff on deck and below, or climbing up the ladders. He was fascinated with the hustle and bustle at the docks, people moving barrels and crates on and off ships and boats.

John's mother had not been feeling well for some time and she had to cough a lot. Her cousin Elizabeth visited her and was very worried to find her in such poor health. She offered to take his mother to her home in the country immediately to get her away from London's smoke and dirt. Kent with its lovely orchards, fields and the seashore would make her well. The cousin decided that John should not come along and see his suffering mother, rather she felt it would be better for him to stay with friends. Sadly, his mother failed to improve and died of pneumonia within weeks.

The cousin wanted to take John as an orphan, but the Captain decided to marry quickly within a couple of weeks, which foiled her plans. The new stepmother was much younger and had no experience with children. Little John found himself a stranger and lonely and he was placed into a boarding school. A tough, sadistic headmaster ruled over the boys and intimidated them with many chores of work and studies. No fun for a little lonely boy. Two years later, when John was eleven, his father decided that he should leave school and sail with him. That began to change his life, living onboard with rough sailors and their vile language. But he began to see the world, meet different people in various seaports, where his father traded and loaded goods to be brought to England.

When his father returned to England within nine months, he decided against taking him on the next voyage. So John was no longer in school and had time for mischief and fights with the town boys. He would go poaching game on the grounds, which means shooting animals without permission. And he had a few frightening experiences that made him think. Once while riding on a horse, he was thrown off it and landed within inches of a spiked branch that could have gone through his eye. Why was he spared? He had to think of his mother and the admonition she gave him. So he tried to behave, but before long he returned to vandalism with the village ruffians. One day he missed getting on a ship in time to join his friends on deck and he was disappointed, but as he turned to leave, the boat keeled over, drowning the waterman and several of John's friends. Again the question in his mind, why was he spared?

Newton became serious for a while and poured over religious books. While onboard of another ship which landed in Holland, he made a discovery that changed his whole concept of God. He discovered a book in English, entitled "Characteristics", written in 1712 by the author Shaftsbury, who was a deist. John was so taken up with the content that he read and memorized most of the book. His findings were: that the Bible is too general, you have to find your own morals. What is right for one person, may be wrong for another. He thus made up his own religion which freed him to do as he pleased.

Captain Newton was concerned about his renegade son and made arrangements for him to find another ship sailing and trading. Eventually he got involved with ships carrying slaves back to England. They were on a tri-part route, from England to Africa to pick up slaves who were tricked and captured by cruel traffickers. In other words, they made it to three ports, one for the slaves, then cleanup, then loading goods for commerce – and back to the same routine. The slaves were packed like sardines in the lower decks, called the hull of the ship where they stayed for the entire journey in the stench until they got to Bermuda to be sold on the slave market.

Dead bodies were hauled overboard into the sea. Before they arrived, the slaves could get on deck to get cleaned up and rubbed in oil, making their skin shiny for the sale.

This sinful blight of heartless men didn't even phase these traders much, their conscience was so hardened. So was John Newton's depraved nature. If his mother could see him now? When the slaves were off the boat, the sailor crew had to clean and scrub the ship somewhat, so they could load goods, like spices, currants, and other merchandise for England. Newton encountered one of the sailors who was different from the rest. He learned that this man was a godly believer who lived his faith and did not swear like the rest. That annoyed Newton and he treated him harshly, maybe his conscience bothered him. He took him on as a special object of defiance because he wanted to break his faith.

Livingstone got more involved with the natives in Africa and settled in with a tribe, even married an African chief's daughter. He liked the customs and ways of those people and decided to live there. But then his fate turned again, the woman he married told her people to punish him, keep him tied down and torture him.

His captain father lost contact with him for years, but he was still concerned where his son was and how he was doing. Then he would lose touch again with John. Meanwhile John tried desperately to get away from the oppressive African wife and village life. He really wanted to get back to England, but how? He had no means, no money, no way to get on a ship to his homeland. One day he met an English merchant, who was traveling the country. They both wanted to get back, but in their escape they found themselves stuck in some backwater riverland, where no ship would ever come to. Behold, as the merchant looked out over the river mouth he saw a large ship on the horizon.

What would it be doing here? He called in excitement, "John, look there is a ship. Let's make a fire quickly, maybe they can see us", and they lit some wood on the beach. Someone on that ship must have been looking in the same direction. That huge ship was sailing back to England but got lost in backwater and eventually made it out of there, taking John Newton and the merchant friend with them. Was that another coincidence? John didn't think so. His life was much more tragic, eccentric and amazing. Again, I am only sketching some of the events, because that ship-in-time seems to be another of those *God-of-the-Splitsecond* events. Lateron the horrendous storm he experienced onboard of another ship about to sink, when Newton really learned to be serious about the Lord and where he experienced "peace in the storm". It must have given him the words for his song "Amazing Grace." When Newton returned to England, he made every effort to help in freeing slaves from trade and worked together with Wilberforce, the abolitionist. Two people who fought for freedom of men created in the image of God.

(The story about Newton may not be accurate, I mislaid my book by Shaftsbury at the time of this writing.)

85. Dayuma and the Aucas

I believe almost everyone has heard of the fantastic but true story of the five American missionaries to the Auca Indians and their early death in the jungle of South America back in 1956. A date and time we in the Christian community remember as well as the death of President Kennedy in 1966. It was a "shot" heard around the world back then, amplified by the media, television, newspapers and of course, by the Christian radio station HCJB, Quito, Ecuador on the hills of the Andes nearby.

The fateful date was January 8, 1956. LIFE Magazine devoted a whole issue to the story of the five missionaries and their project "Operation Auca". The NATIONAL GEOGRAPHIC wrote extensively about the savage stone-age killers who would spear anyone invading their jungle territory. Their real tribal name is Waorani, I believe, but they are called Auca, meaning savages.

I remember one sentence that read like a banner over the life and vision of one of the missionaries, Jim Elliot, who wrote in his diary:

He is no fool, who gives, what he cannot keep (life)
To gain, what he cannot lose (crown).

I didn't know much more about these Auca martyrs, because I was at that time a young foreign student walking around the campus of TBC in Toronto (now Tyndale College) with my German-English dictionary, having trouble understanding those strange words in our classes, like "propitiation," "justification", "eschatology", and the like. But that sentence of Jim Elliot hit home, remembering my parent's attitude towards freedom from Nazism, Communism, they'd risk anything for that priced possession.

That 2-line motto of Jim Elliot could today be read into the determination of some fanatic Moslem suicide terrorist, throwing away his life to serve Allah and get to that paradise up high and get a reward for it. However, there is a world of difference between a true Christian believer who lives in the presence of a loving, holy God day by day, who lives in the vast domain of Christ's kingdom in every capacity of His Creation, not just some heroic act to be rewarded by some weird orgy up yonder and bought with money?

The Shock Heard Around the World.

These five men were real martyrs, not hateful killers, and their wives were also committed to bringing the good news to those Aucas. They were educated real-life people not some off the wall weirdoes or fanatics. College graduates, Ph.Ds, with a bright future, who chose to forsake all to bring the message of the Gospel to those who have not heard yet. What a waste of young lives, people thought. And they went there without a pension plan, extensive medical insurance, accident- or life insurance, without cell phones, microwaves, TV or computers, just taking the barest necessities. They studied the area and habits of those people thoroughly, learned their language and way of life, as they ministered to the neighboring Quichua Indians, who lived in a settlement in Equador.

Their calling was to bring the Word of God to those unreached savages, who apparently did not have a written language of their own. The Wycliffe Bible Translators, and these five saw their mission in that special task.

Who were Those Five Men?

Peter Fleming, Roger Youderian, Ed McCully, Nate Saints and Jim Elliot, all young, married and fathers, except one of them. They planned to make contact with that mysterious, legendary jungle tribe, known as the Aucas. They studied their language from one member who escaped home to avoid being speared to death. Rachel Saint, sister of the Pilot Nate Saint along with the other linguist missionaries at the Quichua base, used their radio station as a point of contact to the venture. They lived at the mission base at Shandia. Jim Elliot and other men built a school building and houses for the workers.

Rachel Saint, the sister of the pilot, worked with Wycliffe Bible Translators and met a young girl named Dayuma, who escaped from the Auca tribe to avoid being speared by one of the men. She settled in a hazienda where other Indians lived and worked for a Spanish boss. Here we see the first connection of a strange weaving of circumstances, and as it became evident lateron, the hand of *God-of-the-Splitsecond* preparing the way for the Gospel.

Why were the Aucas so hostile to outside contact?

About 200 years ago a priest entered their territory with the Gospel but was killed by them. Then in 1925 greedy plantation hunters for rubber invaded and plundered the area, raped and pillaged the tribe and that made them more resolute to fight any invaders. Also the Shell Oil company explored resources of petroleum by cutting down more trees. How were they going to distinguish exploiters from friends?

In fact, the Aucas believed those "pale people" were the cannibals themselves.

Palm Beach and Terminal City

Nate Saint, the pilot from Missionary Aviation Fellowship, who flew between the various mission stations in the region, one day followed a bright shining river winding its way through the thick jungle. Near the Curaray River he saw a clearing of huts and people at the Auca compound. Nate and Jim decided to fly over this area for about a week to investigate. As the yellow wooden plane circled and lowered its range, they slowly dropped a bucket attached to a rope from the plane. In it were gifts of friendship, ribbons, bobbles, a pot, a machete knife and other things. These natives saw the effort and picked up the gifts. One day they put a parrot into the bucket as a return gift to those men in the plane. Soon the natives got used to them and came out to meet the "yellow bee" as they called it.

Eventually the men called from a loudspeaker in Auca words, "We are friends, we like you." Then they looked for a landing spot and found a wide strip of sand along the Curaray River which they named "Palm Beach". They landed there and built a tree house. The five men had announced that they will come down and asked the Auca villagers to come and meet them at the Curaray River. They saw no one, but felt they were being watched from the thick shrubs nearby. After a long wait and calling into the jungle to invite these people to come, three persons came out, one man, whom they later called "George" and two women, of these a young girl maybe sixteen years old. They called her "Delilah". A friendly interchange occurred and they gave these three Aucas more gifts, like rubber bands, and had them try some hamburger and lemonade. Jim was daring and waded through the shallow river to the other side. One couldn't be sure, were they decoys for the warriors behind the trees or a real effort to get to know the flying strangers? George, the older Auca Indian offered young "Delilah" as a gift to the men, but they were not interested.

Instead, "George" got interested in going for a ride in the Piper plane. As they flew, he excitedly gesticulated to the villagers below and calling in his language. He had never seen such wide views or the horizon, in fact. So exited, when they landed, he wanted to fly again, up they went to return once more to Palm Beach.

As sudden as the three came, they disappeared in the jungle. The next day, Sunday, January 8, was the day they expected the village people to come and meet them. It would take the missionaries four hours to make it to Palm Beach. The five were in touch by radio with the home base which Marj Saint operated at Arajuno. The men promised to call back at 4:30 pm hoping to have more good news for them. But no radio message came, it was so unlike them to forget or be late with the radio contact. Something must be wrong, and the world knows the rest of the sad story. Flying over Palm Beach they found a tattered yellow plane, and bodies floating in the river. What went wrong?

It is through several books, which the widow Elisabeth Elliot wrote for our Christian community, one of them entitled "Through Gates of Splendor" (by Tyndale House, 1956, 1957, and 1981) that we get a glimpse of the background to this event and tragedy. What is amazing is the quiet peaceful spirit in which the five widows took the news. And that massacre also affected nine children, most of them small babies. One of them, the 11-year old son Steve Saint who watched his father take off in that wooden Piper plane many times to fly supplies over the jungle or help other missionaries in isolated places. Their composure and deep faith rested in the Almighty God, to whom they entrusted their lives, with or without their husbands, who often sang:

We rest on Thee, our Shield and our Defender,
Thine is the battle, Thine shall be the praise,
When passing through the <u>pearly gates of splendor</u>
Victors, we rest with Thee through endless days.

This was one of their favorite songs, sung to the tune of "Finlandia" by Sibelius. It also happened to be one of our favorite TBC college hymns. In that year 1956, as a freshman at TBC I met Dixie Dean, the famous accordion player who had been working and playing on the HCJB radio station Quito, Ecuador and he knew the five Auca missionaries. What a coincidence, (please read my stories "Dixie and the Stolen Hohner" and "Appleseeds Square and Elisabeth Elliot").

A couple of years later, Rachel Saint and Elisabeth Elliot met two aunts of Dayuma, Mintaka and Mankamu. Dayuma, who was working at the hazienda had not seen them for years and heard about the fate of her brother and the villagers. It is after this encounter that Rachel and Elisabeth moved into the Auca compound with her little 3-year old daughter Valerie. What a daring move, but they were sure the Lord was guiding them to live their lives in love in the midst of those who killed their husbands. The book by Elisabeth, *"The Savage My Kinsman"* is a moving account of their adjustment and witness of living with the Aucas and their love for them. They were the first to enter their territory and lived to tell the story.

What was the mystery behind this Tragedy?

I recently read in a book about Jim Elliot, one factor that the missionaries were not aware of until years later. When they showed the three Aucas visitors a photo of Dayuma, the reaction of those natives was that they recognized that girl, but did not communicate until years later. They felt the white men were cannibals because they reduced Dayuma to such a small person (size of photo) and they took it out of their stomach (pants). Wow, nobody knew this feeling, until Dayuma, who had become a Christian since then, moved into the compound and was preaching and teaching them the Gospel.

But how could anyone anticipate that fear, only God could, or was he taken by surprise?

Strangers with no Ears

The Aucas kept talking away, but did not realize that Elisabeth did not understand, they thought she couldn't hear. And when she scribled words and sounds down on her 3x5 index cards, they called it "scratching", they had no concept of writing. God's Book, the Bible eventually translated by Rachel Saint (working on the project for 16 years) with the Indians nearby – which they called the "scratched book".

Little blond Valerie acting as a natural embassador and interpreter of both cultures - in an innocent, humorous way. What an experience. Eventually a delegation of Christian Quichua Indians visited the Aucas and shared with them their faith. They wore clothes, and had learned some ways to improve their lot. By that time, there were hardly any menfolk left in the Auca territory, because of their ongoing spearing and killing. Dayuma was able to communicate with them, what God is like, accommodating some of the stories to meaningful images - like "there won't be any rain," "we will have houses up there for each one."

Choir and Music in the Sky

Another moving discovery was the fact, that when the nine Aucas speared the missionaries at the Curaray River - Palm Beach, they suddenly heard an unusual singing and music in the sky and in the clouds shining beings and a bright light. They had never seen anything like it and were frightened - was that an angelic choir for the martyrs? But the Aucas only knew that they had done something wrong to see that unususal appearance in the sky. Interesting, because Aucas do not sing, only hum one or two monotonous notes to themselves.

About 30 years later, Elisabeth and her daughter visited the Aucas again to see that group carrying on, like long-time friends they were. Meanwhile, they too are carrying the Good News to others. But, as Elisabeth says, that Palm Beach event was only one incident, one event in the history of God reaching down to lost sinners, in the age-old ongoing march of the Church down here. Only eternity will show the whole picture. Those five missionaries were special, **AAA** people, as someone said, who were totally committed to the Lord : Anytime, Anywhere, Anything

We rest on Thee, our Shield and our Defender,
Thine is the battle, Thine shall be the praise,
When passing through the <u>pearly gates of splendor</u>
Victors, we rest with Thee through endless days.

86. Squanto-On-Time

At the end of my book, I want to include an American event that spells out "*God-of-the-Splitsecond*" in a mar-velous way. It is not my story, but it is part of my heritage as a Pilgrim of the Faith and as a New American. In fact, I wouldn't be here without that Plymouth adventure in 1620 and the mysterious circumstances woven around the brave voyage of a small group of English settlers. And no less amazing is the story of a brave Indian, whose life had been prepared in an unusual way to step in as the most significant person in the survival of those devout believers. Because our history has been tampered with and reconstructed to such a degree, we have been led to believe that the Pilgrims owed most of their gratitude to the Indians, or to Squanto who taught them to plant corn, fish and hunt turkey, who galvanized them against the strange wilderness at Cape Cod. Their devotion to God was just a fantasy of their mind and evidence of their insecurity and unfounded fear, as the history books tell us nowadays.

Recently, I studied the background of the history of Plymouth together with my class of 5th and 6th graders. My own knowledge of historic facts was so muddled that I didn't even know the difference between the two Indians, Samoset and Squanto, so I poured over Peter Marshall's book "The Light and the Glory", among other things, to fill in the gaps. I discovered that the Legend of Squanto has more mysterious aspects that cannot be explained apart from the fact, that the Lord of History had a plan for America and her future as He guided people and events to fulfill His purposes. Fortunately, those Pilgrims were avid "note-takers" and keepers of journals, so we don't have to dream up these things, but just gather the facts.

Well, I was fascinated to learn that, while the Lord worked through the circumstances of the Pilgrims, He also intervened and channeled the life of that young Indian, Tisquantum, and that his story began in 1605, some 15 years before he actually met his friends at Plymouth. I also had to adjust my conviction that the Pilgrims merely came to find religious freedom on the shores of "Virginia", their anticipated destination.

They had already escaped from England for freedom's sake to Holland, because of persecution and eventual exile. The actual reason for their voyage were the hardships in Holland and most of all the danger of loosing their children to the havoc of unbelief and worldliness. They had to work very long and hard for meager wages and their strength was decreasing with age. They knew that it was a dangerous adventure to cross the ocean, but they were driven by their understanding that God wanted them to be the "New Jerusalem" in the "Promised Land" and the "City on a Hill".

Their Mayflower Covenant is, in fact, the Magna Carta and pattern for true democracy and our American Constitution.

I don't want to go into great detail, but would we have the determination to do and endure what they did? To be cooped up in a small boat for about 72 days on a diet of dried peas and dried fish and small amounts of stale water?

Our fear of Y2K, a horrible event of a global computer blackout to take place at the turn of year 2000 – didn't happen incidentally, and that is nothing compared to the ordeal of the Pilgrim seafarers, at least what we know from our privileged lifestyle.

Squanto, who was first captured in 1605 by a Captain and taken to England to study the language so he could serve as an interpreter for trade with the Indians, managed to get back to Cape Cod, only to be confiscated by another captain who was going to sell him into slavery. On his stopover in Spain, a monk noticed him and mercifully bought the boy so that he could hide him in the monastery. That's where Tisquantum (or later named Squanto by the Pilgrims) was introduced to the Christian faith. That Indian-trading captain had second thoughts afterwards and ran to the monastery hoping to reclaim his choice captive, but he monk said he didn't know where the Indian was. So Squanto lived in a profound religious environment in Spain. But in his heart was still the dream to get home to his tribe in America. His father was a chief of the Patuxets at Cape Cod.

Eventually, Squanto managed to talk an English merchant into taking him to Britain, hoping from there to get on a ship home to Cape Cod. In England he worked as a servant for a wealthy man who treated him well, made him wear English clothes and learn their culture and language. He acquired a lot of knowledge (sort of an in-house training) and met good people with Christian principles. But he also learned that there are other kind of people, evil ones, liars, and wicked persons. Not like his Indian people being honest and reliable. Squanto was still homesick for his family and tribe at Cape Cod.

After eight years he found a willing captain who hired him as an interpreter and promised to drop him off at his hometown Pymouth. That ship stopped in Maine where the Indian Samoset got onboard who was an avid traveler visiting many Indian tribes along the coast. Squanto got off at Plymouth as agreed, but found his town deserted and discovered a pile of bones and dried out corn at a campsite of his Patuxet tribe.

Despondent and lonely, his reason for living was gone. Wandering about aimlessly, he came to another tribe, whose chief was Massasoit (now Rhode Island). He offered this orphan Indian to stay with them, whose tribe had been wiped out by a plague just four years prior. No other Indians dared to move into that deserted territory. They believed the Great Spirit had cursed that ground.

Enter the 120 Pilgrims on December 6, 1620 – four months later, as they were driven farther north than the navigated Virginia shores. You can sense the drama intensifying, as *God-of-the-Splitsecond* moves in mysterious ways. The Pilgrims' problems with failing ships and delayed departure could have made them give up their plans. Reaching American shore at the tip of the Cape, they sent 10 men out as scouts in a little dingy boat to find a suitable landing spot. But fog blinded them, so they camped on a little land strip, only to discover the next morning that they were in an ideal port nearby, deep enough for the captain to anchor his seagoing ship. Guess where? Plymouth.

It was already cold winter weather, so the only thing they could hurriedly build was the common meeting house, a log structure with port holes and a roof walk for the sentinels to watch out for Indians. The rough winds and cold weather took its toll on these settlers and after a gruesome winter they lost half of their people, whom they buried at night, so that the Indian spies would not become aware of their dwindling number.

One sunny March day, Samoset, the traveling Indian from Maine showed up and greeted them with "Welcome!" in perfect English. From him they learned the story of the devastating plague at Plymouth. He went back to Massasoit's camp and told Squanto of their new neighbors in his hometown. The next week, the Chief came with Samoset and some of his Wampanoag warriors and of course, our friend Squanto. Chief Massasoit had a good visit and signed a 40-year treaty which both parties kept in good friendship. Our Indian Squanto stayed with the Pilgrims, because he found the calling for his life and adopted these people as his own, in fact, he stayed with them until he died many years later.

In the marvelous puzzle of historic events, each of these people played a God-ordained part at the right time. Praise be to *God-of-the-Splitsecond!* I would like to add, why this is part of my story, because I was actually determined NOT to come to the riot-infested America, but in the mid-60's I met a young man from Australia in Toronto, who had a calling to the ministry and he felt led to go to the New England area. We ended up nearby in New Haven, which has become our home ever since. Also, we spent part of our honeymoon at Plymouth.

87. Schaeffer and L'Abri in the Alps

This Swiss story is better than "Heidi" or the Trapp Family story. Instead of focusing on the mere beauty of those snow-covered mountains or the innocence of an orphan child, you can get an insight into a family that reflected the trust in their majestic God who made those gigantic mountains. While I was in Germany in the '60s, I heard about the

Schaeffer family and the ministry of Dr. Francis Schaeffer, but I didn't know about the "cliff-hanging" crises in their lives in the Alps that shaped their future - and the shelter of hope and vision that L'Abri was to become for many a "wanderer" as result of it. Not until I read Edith Schaeffer's book recently. I assume, they didn't waste time talking about it. And Hollywood hadn't discovered them for a film either.

Let me recall the story that impressed me, the "L'Abri Exodus". Dr. Francis Schaeffer and his wife and their two little girls left the pastorate of a large Presbyterian church in the US to go to Europe in the '50s to bring a message of hope to the war-torn continent. They settled in a French canton in Switzerland as a central place of lodging, from which they traveled to various places to speak and teach. Mrs. Schaeffer as a gifted artist and teacher developed visual lesson material for children, etc.

They rented a chalet in the village of Champery in the French part of Switzerland, and their son Franky was born there. Their home became a friendly place for neighbors and visits of a group of girls from a nearby boarding school who enjoyed a chat and spirited discussions around the cozy fireplace. There was a small boarded-up Protestant chapel tucked away in the hills, which had not been used for years. Someone asked if Dr. Schaeffer would hold regular Sunday services for English tourists. One of the hotels was interested in adding this feature to their brochure.

One day, a devastating and surprising news reached their home in the form of a letter from the Swiss Authorities. The Schaeffers were to leave their home and the country of Switzerland within six weeks by March 31, 1955. They were not permitted to settle in any other Canton (province) either. In other words, they were evicted from Switzerland and the reason given was their religious activity. The villagers were stunned, they wrote fine letters and petitions, but to no avail.

Two of their children were quite ill at that time and it seemed like everything was going against them.

Dr. and Mrs. Schaeffer made a trip to Lausanne to speak to the authorities and find out more about that eviction order. One of the officials who interviewed them looked over the papers, saying "Mmmh, Philadelphia, and such-and-such school, interesting". They didn't recognize each other but discovered that they went to the same school. The man was so excited, he phoned his wife and said that he was bringing an old-time friend and his wife home for lunch. That encounter eventually led to a change in the verdict, namely that the matter be studied.

(I hope you won't mind me calling this little incident GDS#1. And I will continue labeling other phases in this story to highlight the adventure in this "cliff-hanging crisis").

Place for Rent?
But the threat was still hanging over their head, they had to leave the chalet and the village by a designated day, March 31. So Francis and Edith were looking to rent some tourist place until further notice, but they couldn't find anything. Time was running out. Edith took a bus to another village but she couldn't find a place they could afford. She even contacted a realtor to help her find a rental. Nothing available, even in this ski resort teaming with tourists and skiers with their outfit over the shoulders, chatting, and heading for their warm fireplace in the resort home. Edith was exhausted, cold and weary from searching, tears came to her eyes, so she looked down hoping the crowds would not notice.

The night before she spent at the bedside of a pregnant mother who needed her presence. After a sleepless night and a futile rent search, she prayed in desperation: "Lord I must find something in the next half hour before my bus will go back home. Only you can help us, I am at the end of myself. And if you want us to live in a slum, or wherever you will, please help us!" Please remember that there was no telephone booth nearby and cell phones had not been invented yet, for Edith to share her desperation with her husband a few villages away!

Suddenly a car slowed down and the driver called: "Madame Schaeffer, fancy seeing you here." It was that same realtor. "And he even remembered my name?" Edith wondered. He said, "I think I have something for you, step into the car and I'll show you." Off they went, downhill to a place she hadn't seen before. They stopped at a place with steep board steps, a large chalet, all closed up because it hadn't been used for years. It had two balconies across the house and inside the musty deserted place were 12 rooms with possibilities. Edith said to the realtor that she would bring her husband to see this house the next day.

She was so excited, but before they parted she remembered to ask him, "Oh, by the way, how much is the rent, Monsieur?" but he replied, "It's not for rent, it's for sale!" Anyway it was decided, that her husband would come to see this chalet the next morning. (*I can see GDS#2 in the making, and there are many more in Edith's book.*)

Edith did not have the courage to tell her husband beforehand that the house he was to look at was not for rent but for sale. He would have refused to spend time and fare on something like that. But on her ride home in the train the day before she asked the Lord to confirm this unusual find and if He wanted them to buy this house, she asked that they would receive $1000 as a sign. What a wild idea! God would have to drop it from the clouds or did He have a more perfect way? More seriously, their question of "staying in Switzerland" was still uncertain. How foolish to buy under such predicament!!

As Edith and Francis hopped onto the bus from their front steps, the mail lady stopped them and gave them a bundle of letters. They didn't get to open them until they were traveling. And what do you know, there were letters from family, friends, and one from whom they had not heard for a long time. Well, there was a check for $1000 and the story is just as amazing. The woman wrote that her husband had some insurance money refunded to him through his employer and they had been wondering what to buy, another car, a little cottage, and whatever idea came to their mind, they had no peace about it.

The Schaeffers and their ministry came to their mind. The couple finally decided that they would give those $1000 to the Schaeffers for them to buy a place (even though at that time they didn't know what predicament the Schaeffers were in). The letter mentioned that they were going to put it in the mail "tomorrow", but somehow one of them said. "Let's just drop it at the post office tonight." *(GDS#3 – if they had delayed until the morning, the $1000 would not have arrived in time for a "sign". Amazing!)*

A local Swiss notary heard about the prospect and wanted to help the "foreigners" make sure that they made a reasonable, safe deal. His findings, the price and the condition of the chalet was excellent. Why not, when God was the realtor here? That notary also heard that there were other serious buyers and that they must hurry and put a down payment on the next day, as he said on the phone to Edith. Another hurdle? She covered the receiver and called over to her studying husband: "Fran, how much cash do we have available for tomorrow? There was a "cookie-jar" with checks, loose money, gifts etc. And lo and behold the required 8,000 franks (exactly 8,011 franks or $2000) were there with that $1,000 check. *(GDS#4 – God is always on time, even when we cannot see it yet)*

The Schaeffers had to produce about $5,000 of down payment by May 31st. By now, they were learning to trust in this amazing adventure. Somebody helped them move their stuff to the new place with a jeep by maneuvering downhill and uphill across the slopes and along roads – a moving truck would not have done it.

The first day they also got a first glimpse of their location, because it had been raining – now as they ate breakfast on the balcony, they were overwhelmed with the gorgeous valley and mountains of the Rhone from their soon to be "house". But they had no telephone, so Edith had to go to the neighbors, two lovely ladies, and ask to use their phone. That's how the neighbors learned about Schaeffer's problem. One of them said, "Oh, we must tell our brother, he will be able to help you." But Edith thought it was cute of them, because she did not know who their brother was – the President of Switzerland (one of the Council of Seven). Another new acquaintance was a gray-haired elderly man who stopped by the chalet often and talked. He too was shocked at the story, "I" will talk to my nephew." The person (Chief of the Bureau des Etranges) eventually had an influence on the eviction. *(GDS#5– would God have had something to do with that move to Huemoz and placing them between neighbors who'd be instrumental in the change of events?)*

In two months they had to have the remaining money available and the family put a "faith-thermometer" on the wall, watching the miraculous growth of the gifts (157 of them). The children were just as excitedly taking part in this and the mail woman bringing the letters which became part of her mission too. Just before Francis Schaeffer and his daughter were to board the bus to make payment for the house, the mail woman hurriedly handed them a bunch of letters. Guess what, all that was needed duly arrived and only $3 short. No other gifts arrived after this deal was done – which is just as amazing. *(GDS#6 – the amount needed in the nick of time).*

L'Abri – Cluster of Shelters at Huemoz

I wish I could enlarge upon the wonderful adventurous life this family lived in the presence of in-and-out visitors and seekers in reliance upon a God who knows and provides. They even resigned from their mission society – to be utterly dependent upon their "daily bread" from the Providence of God. And what a testimony it has been, echoing its mission and vision in other L'Abri homes and centers in England, Holland, Germany, Australia, and the USA.

Another wonderful story is the creation of the chapel. Edith would in her hectic life of caring, cooking, counseling, escape to her "quiet place", down the front steps, around the next hill and sit at a deserted spot near an old chalet and think "Oh, if we had a chapel!" L'Abri had meanwhile become a whole community from the single chalet, but they needed a house of worship and prayer. So that too was in the mind of the Lord, and it was built with many helping hands and the Swiss neighbor who thought to enlarge his old barn and built it into what is known as "Farrel Chapel". The top floor is for study rooms and the bottom overlooking the Alps is the "Kapelle". (*I see this as GDS#7, a gift to L'Abri for worship and study for their ministry*).

88. Fog on the Hudson River - Washington

This story is taken from Peter Marshall's book "The Light and the Glory" (Fleming H. Revell, 1970) quoting from pages 312-314 in the chapter entitled "The Crucible of Freedom".

This story impressed me greatly as one of the *God-of-the-Splitsecond* events during the American Revolution. After the battle in Concord, Mass, the British assembled large troops on Staten Island (near Amsterdam or what is now New York City). They were lining up for the next battle. There were 32,000 men under General Howe, 9,000 of these were German mercenaries. As Washington guessed, the British considered control of New York pivotal in their attack. If they could control the Hudson River they would have it made to cut off forces from the north. And this would split the Colonies in half and destroy their unity.

There was only one thing in the way, the town of Brooklyn, which was held by the Americans on the western side of Long Island. In the morning of August 22, about 15,000 British troops landed on the southeast shore of Brooklyn without any opposition. Three days later they received another reinforcement of another 5,000 Hessians (also Germans). The other side under Washington had merely 8,000 men, and half of these were untrained. If you get the picture, these Colonists had to fight against extreme odds. Within days they diminished to only 5,000 men. Connecticut's Governor Jonathan Trumbull called for more volunteers to join this poor troop.

Five days later, the British had nearly surrounded them left and center and they had to withdraw to the northern tip of Brooklyn. They fought bravely but were outnumbered 3-to-1 and they were low on ammunition. The British would overtake them. But where is God now? General Howe of the British somehow did not proceed with military logic and use his obvious advantage. Evening came, night arrived and no action by the British. Why the delay? Soon they were to witness the most amazing episode in the Revolutionary War!

The next morning, August 28, daybreak rose quietly and hazed in weather, but no action in the enemy's camp of the British. All day it was quiet and the Americans waited for that last blow. None. In the afternoon it began to rain, and it rained, strong wind pelting those hungry and tired Americans.

Row the Boat Ashore

Suddenly Washington had a plan, and it was a desperate gamble but it was better than merely surrender in defeat. He called a council and informed his officers that the entire army was to cross the river off Brooklyn by small boats. At the foot of Manhattan they would join 12,000 additional men. But it was a full mile across the East River, and the officers were skeptical. What would happen if the British spotted them - sure enough, fire and death. But Washington had made up his mind. It so happened that some of his rein-forcement troops from Massachusetts were "oarsmen", people who knew how to use small boats. And this trip had to be done silently, so that the oars would not splash in the water and the enemy would hear them.

Back and forth they went with these boats, but they would still need three hours to get all the men across to Manhattan in this boat evacuation. They were nervous and worried as the day approached. But a very dense fog began to rise, so dense that you could barely see a man from 6 yards away. The fog remained intact over the water, until the last man was brought to shore, with Washington in it. Then it lifted from the region, and the shocked British ran after them and started to fire, but they were out of their range - to be hit.

This fog event was recorded in many a diary and was one of the miraculous interventions, surely a *God-of-the-Splitsecond* intervention.

89. Beecher's "Uncle Tom's Cabin"

The story of the "Little Woman who started the Great War", as President Lincoln called her one day, is another amazing event. The woman by the name of Harriet Beecher-Stowe, a daughter of the famous New England Minister, Lyman Beecher, who had nine children, most of them becoming ministers also.

Harriet began early in her life to develop a literary interest with her apparent gift for writing. She was passion-ately moved to portray the hardships and sufferings of slaves in the South, as she became more involved in the Abolition Movement, which started in the Christian church, not as our secular contemporaries would have us believe. Harriet wrote the book in the dialect of the Black American slaves and portrayed such a moving drama, that the book moved readers around the world.

I remember my mother reading to us from "Uncle Tom's Cabin" in German and we were moved to tears - how could such cruelty exist? And we would sing some of these "Negro-Spirituals". We were some of those Christians who had to go underground to avoid being persecuted by our Nazi overlords.

In my neighborhood I found an interesting plaque at a cemetery and discovered that Harriet Beecher lived in the hills of Guilford nearby.

Lyman Beecher 1775-1863

Famous early American theologian, lived, learned, worshipped in this area with Aunt Benton and Uncle Lot, after mother died, entered Yale at age 16, graduated 1797. Married Roxanne Foote of Guilford, 1798, Father of Henry Ward Beecher, preacher, orator and writer and Harriet Beecher Stove, author of "Uncle Tom's Cabin."

I also discovered that the original home of the Reverend Lyman Beecher stands near the Guilford harbor. It was drawn to that spot from another site by 60 oxen, as the plaque says beside the front door.

90. Peter Marshall - Light and Glory of America

I am getting to the end of my big book, so I only want to highlight some of the people that impressed me. However, time and space does not permit me to list all of those heroes, inventors, brave men and women, leaders, ministers, artists, freedom fighters and others. Especially Peter Marshall's three volumes of American History, the first one being "The

Light and the Glory". Peter is the son of the famous Chaplain Peter Marshall in the Senate during the World War II, whose prayers influenced many on Capitol Hill. Perhaps you have seen the film "A man called Peter", a tribute to his Chaplain-father. The son's contribution is a vital history book with Christian input. As a graduate of Yale University he had access to the original ancient writings of the Pilgrims and the rare literature of the founding period, for example, Governor Bradford's diary and memoirs of other people.

Someone gave me the book "The Light and the Glory" to read. And I remember settling on a couch and pouring over those pages for hours. What a revelation, my knowledge of America heretofore was rather primitive and superficial, much like other people only see the surface or the current scenery. Here in these volumes can you find an intermingling of historical facts along with the Christian influence of the Founders and citizens – leading up to the present age.

Part V

Reflections and Ponderings

*I*n closing, *I would like to summarize my thoughts and align them with the current circumstances we find ourselves in, ten years after 9-11. I have updated my dormant manuscript which is finally being printed this year 2011 by Xulon Press, Inc.*

Why am I dating this book, you might ask. Because events occur in concrete historic settings, while ideas float in philosophical space driven by the rudder of rational thinking and speculative thoughts. Some of the current ideas are expressed in traditionalism, modernism, and lately the post-mod thinking as well as evolutionism. Someone said that we are "born to think", but to think based on the Truth, not just any truth, which will determine our reality.

The stories in this book focus on the journey of one family and the events which are more than coincidences, but divine interventions and protections. I hope you will discover such in your own lives and pass them on to those you love.

As we consider the horrendous destruction caused by the many hurricanes and tornados, we sympathize with those suffering such losses. And we worry about the violence and unrest in many parts of the world today, not at least the government takeover and insurmountable debt and economic depression in our own country. How shall we then live and survive?

91. Writing - the Tool of Discovery

In the early years of my widowhood in the 1980s, my attention was drawn to the need for repair of my Old Victorian house. But I could not afford to hire anyone, so I learned to do things myself with hammer and saw. Maybe this was an unconscious effort to keep me occupied after work at the office, and to help me forget my grief.

Then a family member begged me to write a *Wedding Digest* for a young bride, a German custom to make a simple scrapbook, newspaper or publication that would be a surprise to the couple.

Soon the need for another book came into view. Why not write a book for my late husband's Australian family whom I never met? They live half around the globe from us and our letters were poor illustrators. So I ventured out and desktop-published a book for them on my Mac computer, entitled *"MORROW, Sojourners in America"*. I believe that little book has made the rounds in Sydney and Tasmania as a "paper visitor" to my late husband's relatives.

Then, instead of spending my evenings in front of the television, I discovered that books were a better choice and began reading and <u>collecting more books</u>. How stimulating!

Somehow, another matter came up one cold winter day that led me into new phase of writing. Some valuable photos of our family were missing which neither I nor my sisters in Germany or Canada could find. Before I realized, I had taped large white posters on my kitchen walls and scotch-taped photos on them in groups. The room looked like a printshop, but who cares?

I ended up mounting them on pages and typing descriptions underneath, then I copied these montages at Kinkos store – five sets. That was all I would do. Each one of my four sisters was going to contribute her part of the text to this volume. Nothing happened.

So I ended up writing the text of our family book on 250 years of history in Eastern Europe, and called it *"The Strauss Chronicles"*. I felt sorry for the money I had spent on the photo montages. But as I look back, I can see that I must have put in the effort to pay a tribute to my deceased parents who had given so much to us. It seems like a "tombstone in writing" to their memory and heroism during World War II and thereafter.

Then another prompting from one of my nieces, to "please, write down those stories for our children", meaning I should compose the various family events that happened in our turbulent lives during the Nazi regime and the refugee years in West Germany, among others. She and her generation were born in post-war luxury and ease. Well, I started with a simple booklet containing about 20 stories. "Is that all?" my niece Anita complained.

And thus came into being my huge manuscript of 250 pages with stories about unusual events, and it is called *"God-of-the-Splitsecond"* (or the GDS-book). I was prompted to number each story and give it a title plus drawing some sketches to illustrate each story. This book went through several revisions since 1996 which I desktop-published and assembled, meaning I had to copy each page and put it into a spiral binder by hand. It would never reach the market and be too time-consuming.

I even had the GDS book copyrighted, but I lost hope of ever having it published, until last fall, when a Publisher actually found me through an email he sent to me. I am presently working on editing the text for publication this year 2011 by Xulon Press, Inc., almost 15 years after the initial inception!

92. "What is that Tool in your Hand?

I don't remember if Moses was asked that question. But I do remember that I became increasingly aware of the tool I have been using for years as a trained stenographer, which helped me to write things down quickly without much distraction. Speedwriting.

Furthermore, I recently discovered an elaborate website called "EasyScript.com" which claimed to hold the secret to fast writing for anyone, any company, even the Fortune 500s.

Well, I compared their method and system with my own phonetic shorthand and found it rather awkward and distracting.

Otaspeed Writing™ came into being by using Tools that speed up your writing at least three times. Since 3 out of 4 words are short one- or two-syllable words, like *"be, have, get, now*," I made *Flashcards* for these TOOLS. My method is to mix and match by using as many of those short word symbols to gain more time for the longhand words. You couldn't do this on your smartphone and not with EasyScript either, where you have to think about prefix, suffix, and 5 rules before you write down ONE word! Meanwhile, the speaker has moved ahead many sentences without you.

Maybe I came onto the scene too late, because we are now in the middle of an epidemic of **"cellphonitis"** and **"texting"**. All that effort to type with two thumbs and wait for an answer? And that in itself is a distraction. Looking at a small keyboard and pecking away? Where do you file the stuff? And how do you retrieve information when you need it instantly? What if the battery has run down. The Bluetooth only connects you to another phonite.

The latest invention of the ingenious **iPad** by Apple is a real hi-tech marvel and it has more possibilities. It beats the laptop computer, but it also has its limitations, you need to carry it with you all the time. You might not be able to plug it in at "Starbucks Coffee Shop" or elsewhere. What then?

Over against all the technological hype, there is still the ancient time-proven method of using pen and paper quickly before one can turn on the computer, or whatever. You can instantly jot down a comment, an idea or a difficult scientific concept, even some graphics to be worked on later.

I have heard about the **"Pulse Pen"** that can write and draw illustrations for you, while you are sitting in class and the professor speaks. All you need to do is scratch a few words etc. on the paper in front of you, and when you touch that spot after class with your Pulse Pen, it will recall and "talk" the message. Only problem is that one has to use special expensive paper.

Another come-lately marvel is the **"e-reader"** or electronic reader or the "Kindle" which can store thousands of books, so you don't have to drag your library along with you. Nice idea if you want to travel light or tuck it under your bedcover. But I still have to ask, can I download the titles that I want or is there a limit to it, or are some titles even "wiped" out or "verboten"? Mercy! Lately I had a salesrep help me find a category like "philosophy" or even "education". Not there unless the words appear in the title of the book. How limiting. And what about the fun of scribbling along the margins or touching the real thing?

Before all these hi-tech writing inventions, I occupied my mind in creating educational material for teens. I was desktop-publishing games and outlines on "apologetics" (philosophy), utilizing some of the ideas expressed in ID "Intelligent Design". My organization is called "Otawit Institute™, and I shall take up where I left off, now since this GDS book is up and running.

You see, I have searched the horizon of writing possibilities and find, that pen and paper (or any writable surface) is still better than the above praised hi-tech tools. Because our brains cannot keep everything in its memory, unless we write some things down quickly.

And in our time of over-exposure to information, we need to be selective and REDUCE, COMPRESS, or OUTLINE with a bit of handwriting. With **Otaspeed Writing™** you are free to express yourself and are not handicapped with a technical straight-jacket.

Another thought on the subject of writing. Have you noticed the elaborate, colorful and expensive journal books in stores with ruled lines inside and very impressive binding? I have avoided buying them because my words are not final. Do I tear pages out if I changed my mind or do I scratch out the text? There is no way I can replace one bad page with a new one in that journal, particularly if I have been spoiled by the editing features of my LAPTOP.

93. America, my Real Home

Without sounding overly patriotic, I can honestly say that America is my real home. I love its history, its beginning, its Constitution, its people and its amazing opportunities for individuals to follow their dreams and fulfill their purpose in life. And most of all, its determination to defend freedom and to take risks in following your dreams. In Brokow's book "The Greatest Generation" he points out the accomplishments and challenges of Americans. We even call the last century the American Century. So many inventions and research efforts have helped people to make life more worthwhile. I myself have spent more of my life in this country than anywhere else, more than forty years. New England is really my home.

However, **We-the-People** may have become used to the opportunities and privileges we have in our country and have let things slide, before we realized the erosion and corruption in our government and elsewhere. It's time again to stand up for principles and get involved in setting things right where we can and should. Most of all, to turn to our Lord and humbly commit ourselves to Him to turn the tide. As millions of average citizens have expressed lately in 2009 and 2010 in the TEA Party Movement, that they object to out-of-control spending and regulations of a Nanny State. Even the Liberty Statue at the Golden Gate would shed tears about the present condition of our Independence.

As a New American in New England I join in the chorus of this beloved anthem, especially since this GDS book "God of the Splitsecond" has been completed for the publisher on this weekend of the Fourth of July:

America the Beautiful
O beautiful for spacious skies,
for amber waves of grain,
for purple mountain majesties
above the fruited plain!
America! America! God shed His grace on thee
And crown thy good with brotherhood,
From seas to shining sea.

94. Fare-Thee-Well Memoirs in my Sunset Years
I should add a few lines to keep in step with the changes and developments of the last decades that have affected my own life. I have penned down some of my thoughts in a private journal, which I call "Fare-Thee-Well". But I do not want to be verbose in writing here about my simple life. Nevertheless, as I am approaching the 80s and in looking back, life seems like a rainbow of colors and experiences, folly, failures and yet wisdom and faith.

A few years ago, I purchased Malcolm Muggeridge's autobiography, entitled "Chronicles of Wasted Time". He was such a gifted person, who accomplished so much in his lifetime as a journalist and ambassador of goodwill. I was intrigued by the seemingly unfitting title for this British hero. Why I finally gave up reading his 1000 page volume was that it contained neither an index nor outline, and I could not find anything again after I had read it. It began to waste my time. I must watch that I don't waste words about my own rather obscure life. That's why I segmented my life story in the GDS family book into short narratives.

As I mentioned in the outline of my book, I found a trilogy of themes which I describe as:

*** three caravans * three ships *three centuries**

The first two are part of our unique family experience in Europe and Canada, but the third theme may be yours as well, if you are in my age group. It is a unique generational experience for people born in the 1920s and thereafter. In fact, we are the first people in human history who have gone through such vast and rapid changes in one lifetime. Our ancestors lived and died in one era, but we had to adjust to three:

19th Century– the field and the oil lamp -*agriculture*
20th Century– the electricity and the assembly line - *industry*
21st Century– the atom bomb and the computer chip - *hi-tech*

That cultural gap closes again, if you were born in the post- agricultural period, then you only adjusted to the other two (the industrial and the hi-technology) eras. Indeed an interesting observation.

My parents actually lived in the first two centuries. My father died of cancer at the age of 75 years. At that time, there were only a few large computers by IBM and Honeywell and they took up the space of a room in some large company or government office. But dad as a one-time teacher and philosopher was an avid writer all his life with beautiful penmanship (neat looking handwriting), pages and pages of text still in the old Gothic German script. He would have loved to own a computer or laptop where he could edit to his heart's content rather than scribbling corrections. It reminds me of what I heard once:

> *"If Moses would have had a computer instead of tablets of stone, the TEN COMMANDMENTS would not have been better – only lighter."*

Some of our kids think, the only thing that matters is the present, even the present moment. But they are wrong, because education is supposed to give us the scope for our entire human history and how it affects our lives. We might think today of "history and science" as the main source of knowledge. But there are layers of our understanding. It used to be theology, then it became philosophy and then psychology. Knowledge and education is supposed to widen our horizon and help us build like a pyramid on the achievement of previous generations.

Someone said, "If we don't know history, we are doomed to repeat it." And another said, "If we don't know where we have been, then we don't know where we are, and we don't know where we are going to." A bit of philosophy of human thought and action. We used to call this department of studies "Liberal Arts" in our colleges. But it has nothing to do with liberal politics or with modern art, whatsoever.

95. Yesterday-Today-Tomorrow

Our yesterdays define our todays to an extent, but they don't necessarily have to determine our future as well, because we often have choices and decisions to make. While I was basically describing our family, I cannot help thinking about the countless families and individuals who became victims of evil tyranny and war as well. About eleven millions refugees and political prisoners were uprooted from their homes in the last century. Every 4th person in Germany is a refugee (or now a descendant of one). In addition to those millions, about 60 million people have been killed by Communism and Nazism in Europe. What devastation, what disgrace to the dignity of the human race! We as survivors blissfully lived our lives in the post-war and cold-war years both in Europe and here in America.

And the "Chocolate Pilot" dropping his sweet parachutes from his plane to a city completely destroyed by bombs, reminds me somehow of the devastation caused by hundreds of natural disasters during this year 2011, when Joplin, Mississippi and many other places were razed to the ground by tornados, or others were flooded by great hurricanes. When everything is gone, what remains in your life?

Equally as worrisome is the tremendous change our United States has undergone for several years now by extensive government takeover and control and insurmountable debt. How are we going to survive and resist that? We need to rely on the hope and strength of our Lord, the God of our Fathers, in this critical time, to stand and defend our freedoms.

My thoughts turn again to the idea of the ocean of life and the ship in which we are sailing along, and I want to close with this prayer:

MAY OUR LIVES
carry the cargo entrusted to us,
the experiences lived, the tasks given,
the friends cherished, the people served
be to the GLORY OF GOD
and may He bring us to our
HEAVENLY SHORE.

Bibliography

\# 77   Berlin Exodus through the Red Sea
         Peter and Elfriede Dyck, *"Up From The Rubble"*,
         Herald Press, Scottsdale, PA, 1991

\# 79   Hansi, Orphan Girl for Hitler
         Maria Anne Hirschmann, *"Hansi, The Girl Who
         Loved The Swastika"*, Tyndale House Publishers,
         Wheaton, IL, 1973.

\# 80   Corrie ten Boom at the Prison Gate
         Corrie ten Boom, *"Watchmaker's Daughter"*,
         Fleming H. Revell Co., Old Tappan, NJ, 1982.

\# 81   Freedom Dance – Bolshoi Ballet
         Dallas L. Barnes, *"Freedom Dance"*, Here's Life
         Publishers, San Bernardino, 1985.
         (now assigned to Tyndale House Publishers)

\# 85   Dayuma and the Aucas
         Elisabeth Elliot, *"The Savage My Kinsman"*,
         Servant Books, Ann Arbor, 1961, 1989.
         Ethel Emely Wallis, "The Dayuma Story", Life
         under Auca Spears. Harper & Bros.
         Publishers, New York, 1960.

86   Squanto-on-Time for the Pilgrims
Peter Marshall, David Manuel, *"The Light and the Glory"*, Fleming H. Revell, Division
of Baker Book House, 1977.
Focus on the Family: *"The Legend of Squanto"*,
Radio Theater Tape Edition, 1999.

87   Schaeffer and L'Abri in the Alps
Edith Schaeffer, *"L'Abri"*, Tyndale House
Publishers, Wheaton, IL, 7th Edition, 1973.

#90   Peter Marshall and David Manuel, "The Light and the Glory", Fleming H. Revell, 1977.

On the Collapse of Communism:
Michael Bourdeau, *"The Gospel's Triumph over Communism"*, Bethany House Publishers,
Minneapolis, MN 1991.
Bud Bultman, *"Revolution by Candlelight"*, Multnomah,
Portland, 1991.
Barbara von der Heyd, *"Candles behind the Wall"*,
Wm. B. Eerdmann Publishing Company etc., Grand
Rapids, 1993.

On the Caravans and Ancestors:
Ernst Hobler and Rudolf Mohr, editors, *"Vor 200 Jahren aus der Pfalz nach Galizien und in die Bukowina"*,
Report for the 200. Anniversary. published by the
Hilfskomitee of the Galizia-Germans, Stuttgart-Bad
Cannstadt, 1982.

Permission to use two linoleum cuts by Rudolf Unterschütz given by Horst Vocht, President of Hilfskomitee of Galizia-Germans.
1) caravans on the road, and 2) colonists resting under an oak.

CPSIA information can be obtained at www.ICGtesting.com
Printed in the USA
BVOW010459090212

282546BV00001B/6/P